My Name Is Legion

To Pam Tyng,
Grace to you &
peace!

Michael W
Newheart
7 Nov 04

INTERFACES

Series Editor: Barbara Green, O.P.

"My Name Is Legion"

The Story and Soul of the Gerasene Demoniac

Michael Willett Newheart

A Michael Glazier Book

LITURGICAL PRESS

Collegeville, Minnesota

www.litpress.org

A Michael Glazier Book published by the Liturgical Press

Cover design by Ann Blattner. Watercolor by Ethel Boyle.

1	2	3	4	5	6	7	8

Library of Congress Catalog-in Publication Data

Newheart, Michael Willett, 1955–
    My name is Legion : the story and soul of the Gerasene demoniac /
Michael Willett Newheart.
        p. cm. — (Interfaces)
    "A Michael Glazier book."
    Includes bibliographical references and index.
    ISBN 0-8146-5885-7 (pbk. : alk. paper)
    1. Healing of the Gerasene demoniac (Miracle) 2. Bible. N.T. Mark V,
1–20—Psychology. 3. Bible. N.T. Mark V, 1–20—Criticism, Narrative.
I. Title. II. Series: Interfaces (Collegeville, Minn.).

BT367.H38N49 2004
226.7'06—dc22   2004009065

Writing a book is a horrible, exhausting struggle, like a long bout of some painful illness. One would never undertake such a thing if one were not driven on by some demon whom one can neither resist nor understand.

George Orwell[1]

PRAYER TO LEGION

O Legion

Come to me

Possess me

Distress me

Oppress me

Do not come out

'til this book is out

And then

I shall be healed

Michael Willett Newheart

[1] Quoted in Glenn Frankel, "A Seer's Blind Spots; On George Orwell's 100th, a Look at a Flawed and Fascinating Writer," *The Washington Post* (Washington, DC: June 25, 2003) C1.

To the men of

the Maryland Correctional Institution at Jessup (MCIJ)

and

the women of

the Maryland Correctional Institution for Women (MCIW)

who have participated in

Alternatives to Violence Project (AVP) Workshops.

May your tribe increase.

CONTENTS

Preface xi

Acknowledgments xv

Introduction: Reading the Story, Probing the Soul xvii

Part I
Reading the Gerasene's Story: Narrative Criticism 1

CHAPTER ONE
Tell Me the Old, Old Story: The Gospels as Narratives 3

CHAPTER TWO
Mark My Word: The Story of the Crucified Son of God 18

CHAPTER THREE
Recovering from "Legionnaire's Disease":
The Story of the Gerasene's Exorcism 34

Part II
Probing the Gerasene's Soul: Psychological Biblical Criticism 51

CHAPTER FOUR
Legion's Unconscious Uncovered: Freud and Jung 53

CHAPTER FIVE
Legion Scapegoated and (De)Colonized: Girard and Fanon 70

CHAPTER SIX
Reading Legion's Story with (New)Heart and Soul 86

Conclusion: Telling the Story, Enriching the Soul 105

Bibliography 111

Appendix: Poems on the Gerasene 117

Scripture Index 123

PREFACE

The book you hold in your hand is one of ten volumes in a new set. This series, called INTERFACES, is basically a curriculum adventure, a creative opportunity in teaching and learning, presented at this moment in the long story of how the Bible has been studied, interpreted, and appropriated.

The INTERFACES project was prompted by a number of experiences that you, perhaps, share. When I first taught undergraduates, the college had just received a substantial grant from the National Endowment for the Humanities, and one of the recurring courses designed within the grant was called Great Figures in Pursuit of Excellence. Three courses would be taught, each centering on a figure from some academic discipline, with a common seminar section to provide occasion for some integration. Some triads were more successful than others, as you might imagine. But the opportunity to concentrate on a single individual—whether historical or literary—to team teach, to make links to another pair of figures, and to learn new things about other disciplines was stimulating and fun for all involved. A second experience that gave rise to the present series came at the same time, connected as well with undergraduates. It was my frequent experience to have Roman Catholic students feel quite put out about taking "more" biblical studies, since, as they confidently affirmed, they had already been there many times and done it all. That was, of course, not true; as we well know, there is always more to learn. And often those who felt most informed were the least likely to take on new information when offered it.

A stimulus as primary as my experience with students was the familiarity of listening to friends and colleagues at professional meetings talking about the research that excites us most. I often wondered: Do her undergraduate students know about this? Or how does he bring these ideas—clearly so energizing to him—into the college classroom? Perhaps some of us have felt bored with classes that seem wholly unrelated to research, that rehash the same familiar material repeatedly. Hence the idea for this series of books to bring to the fore and combine some of our research interests with our teaching and learning. Accordingly, this series is not so much about creating texts *for* student audiences but rather about *sharing* our scholarly passions with them. Because these volumes are intended each as a piece of original scholarship, they are geared to be stimulating to both students and established scholars, perhaps resulting in some fruitful collaborative learning adventures.

The series also developed from a widely shared sense that all academic fields are expanding and exploding, and that to contemplate "covering" even a testament (let alone the whole Bible or Western monotheistic religions) needs to be abandoned in favor of something with greater depth and fresh focus. At the same time, the links between our fields are becoming increasingly obvious as well, and the possibilities for study that draw together academic realms that had once seemed separate is exciting. Finally, the spark of enthusiasm that almost always ignited when I mentioned to students and colleagues the idea of single figures in combination—interfacing—encouraged me that this was an idea worth trying.

And so with the leadership and help of Liturgical Press Academic Editor Linda Maloney, as well as with the encouragement and support of Editorial Director Mark Twomey, the series has begun to take shape.

Each volume in the INTERFACES series focuses clearly on a biblical character (or perhaps a pair of them). The characters from the first set of volumes are in some cases powerful—King Saul, Pontius Pilate—and familiar—John the Baptist, the patriarch Joseph; in other cases they will strike you as minor and little-known—the Cannibal Mothers, Herodias. The second "litter" emerging adds notables of various ranks and classes: Jezebel, queen of the Northern Israelite realm; James of Jerusalem, "brother of the Lord"; Simon the Pharisee, dinner host to Jesus; Legion, the Gerasene demoniac encountered so dramatically by Jesus. In any case, each of them has been chosen to open up a set of worlds for consideration. The named (or unnamed) character interfaces with his or her historical-cultural world and its many issues, with other characters from biblical literature; each character has drawn forth the creativity of the author, who has taken on the challenge of engaging many readers. The books are designed for college students (though we think they are suitable for seminary courses and for serious Bible study), planned to provide young adults with relevant information and at a level of critical sophistication that matches the rest of the undergraduate curriculum. In fact, the expectation is that what students are learning of historiography, literary theory, and cultural anthropology in other classes will find an echo in these books, each of which is explicit about at least two relevant methodologies. It is surely the case that biblical studies is in a methodology-conscious moment, and the INTERFACES series embraces it enthusiastically. Our hope is for students to continue to see the relationship between their best questions and their most valuable insights, between how they approach texts and what they find there. The volumes go well beyond familiar paraphrase of narratives to ask questions that are relevant in our era. At the same time, the series authors also have each dealt with the notion of the Bible as Scripture in a way condign for them. None of the books is preachy or hortatory, and yet the self-implicating aspects of working with the revelatory text are handled frankly. The assumption is, again, that college can be a good time for people to reexamine and rethink their beliefs and assumptions, and they need to do so in good company. The INTERFACES volumes all challenge teachers to re-vision radically the scope of a course, to allow the many connections among characters to serve as its warp and weft. What would emerge fresh if a Deuteronomistic History class were organized around King Saul, Queen Jezebel, and the two women who petitioned their nameless monarch? How is Jesus' ministry thrown into fresh relief when structured by shared concerns implied by a demoniac, a Pharisee, James—a disciple, and John the Baptist—a mentor? And for those who must "do it all" in one semester, a study of Genesis' Joseph, Herodias, and Pontius Pilate might allow for a timely foray into postcolonialism.

The INTERFACES volumes are not substitutes for the Bible. In every case they are to be read with the text. Quoting has been kept to a minimum for that very reason. The series is accompanied by a straightforward companion, *From Earth's Creation to John's Revelation. The INTERFACES Biblical Storyline Companion,* which provides a quick overview of the whole storyline into which the characters under special study fit. The companion is available gratis for those using two or more of the INTERFACES volumes. Already readers of diverse proficiency and familiarity have registered satisfaction with this slim overview narrated by biblical Sophia.

The series' challenge—for publisher, writers, teachers, and students is to combine the volumes creatively, to INTERFACE them well so that the vast potential of the biblical text continues to unfold for us all. These ten volumes offer a foretaste of other volumes currently on the drawing board. It has been a pleasure to work with the authors of these first volumes as well as with the series consultants: Carleen Mandolfo for Hebrew Bible and Catherine Murphy for New Testament. It is the hope of all of us that you will find the series useful and stimulating for your own teaching and learning.

Barbara Green, O.P.
INTERFACES Series Editor
May 16, 2004
Berkeley, California

ACKNOWLEDGMENTS

A spiritual says:
How I got over
How I got over
My soul looks back and wonders
How I got over.

I "got over" thanks to a number of people, many of whom are at Howard University School of Divinity, where I teach. I made presentations of various stages of the manuscript at the Faculty Dialogue, to the Faculty Writing Group, and in my classes in Introduction to New Testament I and the Miracles of Jesus. I am grateful to colleagues and students for their comments, questions, and encouragement. I also thank former Dean Clarence G. Newsome for a Faculty Development Grant, funded by the Lilly Endowment, which allowed me to write much of the manuscript in the summer of 2003. I am also grateful to the School of Divinity Librarian Carrie Hackney and her staff for securing for me needed books.

I also thank colleagues in the Synoptic Gospels Section of the Mid-Atlantic regional Society of Biblical Literature, where in spring 2002 I first presented the foundation of what became this book. I appreciate greatly the efforts of those who read (quickly) and commented (insightfully) on portions of the manuscript: Whitney Shiner, David Howell, Petri Merenlahti, D. Andrew Kille.

I thank Linda Maloney, Academic Editor at the Liturgical Press, for telling me about Interfaces while my previous book *Word and Soul* was still in press, and Barbara Green, editor of the Interfaces series, for offering her perceptive guidance at the beginning and her careful editing at the end.

Thanks to my psychologist Dorothy Kaplan, my writing coach Mike Thomas, and the men's group at Adelphi Friends Meeting. And many, many—a legion of—thanks to my long-suffering family. Yes, Ana and Miranda, I'm finally done with the book, and Joy, it is primarily because of you that I have gotten over.

An earlier version of chapter five was published as "Legion: A Violent Soul in a Violent Society (Mark 5:1-20)," in J. Harold Ellens, ed., *The Destructive Power of Religion: Violence in Judaism, Christianity, and Islam* (Westport, CT: Praeger, 2004) 2:199–217. I am grateful to the editor and to Praeger for permission to publish it here in a revised form.

INTRODUCTION
Reading the Story, Probing the Soul

"My name is Legion, for we are many."

This is what I said back when I was demonized, back when I had an unclean spirit—a legion of them actually. This is what I said when Jesus asked me my name. You've probably heard of that saying. I hear it used often in your day.

Let me tell you my story. I had a legion of demons, or unclean spirits, as the Jews said. How did I get them? I don't know. But I know that I was in torment. I roamed the mountains and the graveyards. I felt dead. People tried to chain me, to bind me. I don't know why. They were afraid of me for some reason. It seems that I was living their anger, their frustration. I became so frustrated at Roman occupation. I just went crazy! CRAZY! The legions occupying our land became demonic and occupied my body and my soul.

I went out to the mountains to be among the dead. I was dead. I wanted to kill myself, to gash myself, to kill the demons. The people, the people tried to bind me, to chain me, to put chains on my wrists and fetters on my ankles. But these demons, these unclean spirits made me strong, SO STRONG that I tore apart TORE APART the chains and SMASHED the fetters! Oh, sorry. I was getting a little carried away there. A little carried away. I guess I got "re-possessed."

I would roam, roam the mountains . . . and HOWL. Howl! Like a wild animal, a wild animal. That's what I was. I would take the stones and cut myself, gash myself, slash myself. I was miserable.

One day, though, I saw this guy come ashore from a boat across the sea. I somehow knew him. He was Jesus, a powerful spirit man. I was both drawn to him and repelled by him. I had to go to him. I had to get rid of him. So I ran to him, and I fell down at his feet. He had a spirit that was stronger than all the spirits inside me. I screamed at him. (I only knew how to do things in a big way.) I screamed at him, "WHAT'VE YOU GOT AGAINST ME, JESUS SON OF THE HIGHEST GOD?" I recognized that he was not just a son of a god, but the son of the highest god. This YHWH God, this God of the Israelites. It was by that God, by that God, that I swore, I swore. I swore to him, "DON'T TORTURE ME!" I wasn't thinking about the torture I was giving to myself. Only what he would do to me.

It seemed he was about to tell the unclean spirit to leave, but instead he asked my name, my name. I said, I said, "My name is Legion. My name is Legion. For we, for we are many." Then I begged him wildly WILDLY not to send, not to send, not to send the demons out of the region. This Roman legion possessed the land. I did not want them to leave.

I saw pigs grazing on the hillside. Pigs. The people raised them to feed the troops that were stationed in the village. Pigs for the Roman pigs! The spirits asked Jesus to send them into the pigs. And he did it. He did it! The demons left me. They left me and went into the pigs. And those pigs started acting CRAZY! Rather than acting like pigs and scattering in all directions, they acted like sheep, like lemmings, and ran together as a herd off a bank and plunged into the lake. And they drowned. Oh, I bet there were 2000 pigs.

As the pigs ran into the sea, the people tending them ran into the city and into the country to tell what had happened. And people came running to see. They came to Jesus, and they saw me. I was sitting down, not roaming around the graves and the mountains. I was dressed, not naked. And I was sane, not crazy, not possessed.

And the people were afraid. They knew that something spirited, spiritual, spiritually powerful had happened. What did this mean? How would the demonic Roman legions react when their food supply was now in the bottom of the lake? What would the people do with their rage now that I would no longer carry it for them? And what would they do with the divine, the highest god, who was now making himself known?

Those who saw what happened to me told the others what had happened to the pigs. And they asked Jesus to get out of town! They wanted to run him off into the sea. They had worked out a nice little arrangement with the Romans, using me as their scapegoat. Now that was all dead. And I was alive.

So Jesus agreed to leave. As he was getting into the boat, I ran to him again. This time, though, I wanted to be with him. I didn't want to be with these people who had shackled me both literally and figuratively. I wanted to be bound to Jesus. I wouldn't break those bonds. I wanted to follow him. So I asked him if I could go with him, be one of his disciples. But he refused. He told me to go home to my people and tell them what the Lord, the highest God of the Jews, had done for me and how he had had compassion on me. At first I was disappointed. You want me to go back to the people who had shunned me, upon whom I had brought incalculable shame!? But I thought,

Hey, I would not go home; I would go to the whole province, not just Gerasa but to all the Ten Cities, and tell them what Jesus had done for me.

And that's what I did. And you should have seen those people in the Ten Cities. Their eyes bulged, and their jaws dropped. They were amazed!

So that's my story. Pretty wild, isn't it?

Mark's Version of the Story (5:1-20)

Here is how my story is told in a book you know as the Gospel of Mark. My friend Michael Newheart has translated it from the original, which was written in Greek. He will pick up the comments following the story.

And they came to the other side of the sea,
to the region of the Gerasenes.
And when Jesus got out of the boat,
suddenly there met him out of the tombs
a man with an unclean spirit,
who was living among the tombs,
and no one could restrain him any longer,
not even with a chain,
for he'd been bound with fetters and chains many times,
but the chains were torn apart by him and the fetters smashed,
and no one was strong enough to tame him.
And every night and day
among the tombs and on the mountains
he was screaming
and gashing himself with stones.

And when he saw Jesus from a distance,
he ran and fell down in front of him,
and he screams with a great voice and says,
    "WHAT'VE YOU GOT AGAINST ME,
    JESUS SON OF THE HIGHEST GOD?
    I SWEAR TO YOU BY GOD,
    DON'T TORTURE ME!"
For Jesus was about to say to him,
    "Come out of the man, you unclean spirit!"
And Jesus asked him,
    "What's your name?"
And he says to him,
    "Legion's my name,
    for we're many."
And he begged Jesus wildly not to send them out of the region.

Now on the mountainside was a great herd of pigs grazing.
And the spirits begged him,
    "Send us into the pigs,
      so we can enter them."
And he let them.
And the unclean spirits went out of the man and into the pigs.
And the herd,
about two thousand strong,
rushed down a steep bank into the sea,
and they were drowned in the sea.

And those grazing the pigs ran off
and told what had happened
in the city and the country,
and people came to see.
And they come to Jesus,
and they see the demonized one,
the man who had had the legion,
seated, dressed and sane,
and they were afraid.
And those who had seen what had happened to the demonized one
also recounted to them about the pigs.
And they began begging Jesus to get out of their country.
And as he got into the boat,
the ex-demonized one begged Jesus to be with him,
but Jesus didn't let him;
rather, he says to him,
    "Go home to your own people,
      and tell them what the Lord has done for you
      and how he's had compassion on you."
And the man left and began preaching in the Ten Cities what Jesus
    had done for him,
and everyone was amazed.

My Personal Attraction to the Story

You've heard from the Gerasene and from Mark. Now it's time you heard from me, Michael Willett Newheart, the author of this book. Indeed, you will hear my voice for the rest of the book.

For some years now I've been attracted—one might even say "possessed"—by the Gerasene of Mark 5:1-20, the man whose legion of demons are cast out by Jesus. Back in the mid-80s when I had my first teaching post in a small Baptist liberal arts college, I would often perform dramatic monologues of biblical characters, and the Gerasene was one of my favorites. (I portrayed him as he was after the exorcism rather than before!) I occasionally took him "on the road" when I was asked to preach in local Baptist churches. He was always quite a hit! In 1991 the American Bible Society produced a nine-minute video of this passage, which turned out to be sort of an "MTV" version. When I first saw it at a professional meeting of biblical scholars, I was transfixed. I made sure that the library at Howard Divinity had it, and I have often shown it in class.

Now, over a decade later, I have written a book on this passage in the Liturgical Press's INTERFACES series, which focuses on biblical personalities. (The Gerasene, with a legion of demons, has more personalities than anybody in the Bible!)

Why does the Gerasene intrigue me so? He is the wild man. I am the good divinity school Bible professor. Through him I live my wildness, my shadow, to use Jungian terms. But I also long for the healing he experienced. I have my own demons, though I usually do not name them as such. I suffer from generalized anxiety disorder (GAD) and depression, for which I am medicated and participate in psychotherapy. As I read of his exorcism, I experience vicariously being "in my right mind" (Mark 5:15).

I am also compelled by the violence of the passage. The Gerasene is someone who had to carry the violence of his people, yet Jesus delivered him from the violence. For over two decades I have been active in the peace movement, culminating in my recently becoming a Quaker, a member of the Religious Society of Friends, which has stood against violence since its inception in seventeenth-century England. My interpretation of the passage, then, is shaped by my commitment to nonviolence.

What Readers Can Expect from This Book

This is a book for undergraduates. I'm certainly happy for anybody to read it, but the book was written for college and university students in classes on the Bible or New Testament. It focuses on the Gospel of Mark, the document that appears second in the New Testament. Within Mark it focuses on one character, the Gerasene demoniac, who appears in one story in the gospel, the story of his exorcism quoted above. (Versions of the story also appear in the gospels of Matthew 8:28-34 and Luke 8:26-39. I will discuss them only in passing because my focus is on Mark.) I approach the story from the perspective of two scholarly methods: narrative criticism and psychological biblical criticism. You've probably already looked at the table of contents, so you have some idea of the way I'm going to proceed in this book. The book is divided into two parts. In the first I deal with narrative criticism, and in the second I deal with psychological criticism. With narrative criticism, I go from general to specific. I discuss the gospels as stories (Chapter 1), then Mark as a story (Chapter 2), and finally the story of the Gerasene's exorcism (Chapter 3). With psychological biblical criticism I take a somewhat different tack. I discuss five different psychological approaches to the story: those inspired by Sigmund Freud and Carl Jung (Chapter 4), those inspired by René Girard and Frantz Fanon (Chapter 5), and my own soul reading (Chapter 6). A conclusion will wrap things up.

This book is written in plain language. It is not written from a sectarian standpoint. Although I am a Christian and a Quaker, I am respectful of those who follow different paths, as well as those who do not follow any path.

What I Can Expect of You, the Reader

Just as you expect some things from me, I expect some things from you. I expect you to read the Gospel of Mark with me. I would suggest that you first read it silently straight through in one setting. Then I would suggest that you read it aloud in groups. Or maybe you will want to watch a videotape of a dramatic presentation of the gospel, such as the one by David Rhoads.[1] You will find that the story comes alive when it is read on its own, without the other gospels interfering. Also, Mark was written to be read aloud, for in the first century, when it was written, literacy was relatively low, and the price of writing and reading materials was high.

I would also suggest that while you're reading this book (and the Gospel of Mark) you also read some fiction, that is, novels or short stories. I know, you're saying, "I already have more than enough to read, thank you, with textbooks and term papers." I know that, but you will have to take some time to unwind, and I think a great way to do that is by reading fiction. You might want to read historical fiction about characters in the Bible. I would recommend *Living Water* by Obery Hendricks, about the Samaritan woman,[2] and two novels about Jesus, one by a novelist and the other by a biblical scholar: *Testament* by Nino Ricci,[3] and *The Shadow of the Galilean* by Gerd Theissen.[4] Or maybe you like short stories. If so, I

---

[1] David R. Rhoads, Dramatic Presentation of the Gospel of Mark. Available from SELECT, 2199 East Main Street, Columbus, OH 43209-2234, http://www.elca.org/dm/select/order.asp?sort=Title.

[2] Obery Hendricks, *Living Water: A Novel* (San Francisco: HarperSanFrancisco, 2003).

[3] Nino Ricci, *Testament* (Boston: Houghton Mifflin, 2003).

[4] Gerd Theissen, *The Shadow of the Galilean: The Quest of the Historical Jesus in Narrative Form* (Philadelphia: Fortress, 1987).

would suggest a collection of African-American short stories such as *Breaking Ice*, edited by Terry McMillan,[5] *Black American Short Stories*, edited by John Henrik Clarke,[6] and *The Best Short Stories by Black Writers*, edited by Langston Hughes.[7]

I would encourage you to keep a journal. It would include notes, questions, and insights, but it would also include drawings and poetry. I would also urge you to talk about what you learn with others. You simply retain the information longer if you discuss it with another person. Choose someone outside of the class, and meet with that person regularly so that you can talk about what you're learning in the class.

I hope that reading this book will be fun. I hope it will be interesting. Biblical studies have been both fun and interesting for me. They have even been transformative. I hope you are transformed in reading this book and the Gospel of Mark. Specifically, I hope you will become more critical, creative, and compassionate. By "critical" I mean that I hope you are more reasoned, intelligent, thoughtful, and reflective in reading biblical texts. By "creative" I mean that I hope you will use art, drawing, poetry, music, and drama in responding to the stories we discuss. By "compassionate" I mean that I hope you are more loving toward yourself and the world, more committed to build up community, more committed to peace and justice, and more committed to use religious texts in order to do that.

Just as Jesus and his disciples went to the other side of the sea to meet this demon-possessed man, let us, too, go to the other side!

---

[5] Terry McMillan, ed., *Breaking Ice: An Anthology of Contemporary African-American Fiction* (New York: Penguin, 1990).

[6] John Henrik Clarke, ed., *Black American Short Stories: One Hundred Years of the Best* (New York: Hill and Wang, 1993).

[7] Langston Hughes, ed., *The Best Short Stories by Black Writers: The Classic Anthology from 1899 to 1967* (New York: Little, Brown, 1967).

PART I
Reading the Gerasene's Story: Narrative Criticism

CHAPTER ONE

Tell Me the Old, Old Story: The Gospels as Narratives

Let me begin with a story.

Got your attention, didn't I? You thought I was going to tell you a story, not just some dusty old theory, but a story about people with juice and guts and glory. You became interested, didn't you?

Our lives are "storied": that is, stories give structure to human life. Muriel Rukeyser said it well: "The universe is made up of stories, not atoms."[1] Whenever we want to tell people who we are, we tell a story. I have a friend named Ben who has been teaching classes via teleconference for several years. He likes to have his students get to know one another well, yet he realizes that a teleconference class presents problems because participants cannot see faces or shake hands. All people have is the voice. Usually he begins by having everyone talk about what they expect from the class. Recently, though, Ben decided to try something different. He had them each write a three-hundred-word story about themselves. He told them they had to have a beginning, middle, and end. At the next class some of the students read their stories, and all of them were quite powerful. This "story approach" turned out to be a highly effective way to introduce the course and students to one another.

We are defined by our stories. This statement is true for us as individuals and for the groups we are a part of. We all have family stories that are passed down from generation to generation. For example, my wife Joy got her middle name Olinia because a man named Olin nursed her great-grandfather Allen Love Williams back to health after a steamboat fire, and Mr.

---

[1] Quoted (without citation) in A. Katherine Grieb, *The Story of Romans: A Narrative Defense of God's Righteousness* (Louisville: Westminster John Knox, 2002).

Williams pledged to name his firstborn after him. The family has passed that name (and story) on down through the years.

I recently asked my children, Ana and Miranda, ages seven and four-and-a-half, respectively, what stories they would tell their grandchildren about me. They both said, "What happened to the groceries?" That story goes like this: Before Miranda was born, I took two-year-old Ana to our local Safeway and purchased a cartful of groceries. Being distracted by profound thoughts (!), however, I absentmindedly left the groceries on the curb while we drove away. When I pulled into our driveway, I realized what had happened, so we backed out and returned to the store, only to find the groceries gone. I went to the help desk, which was no help, for the manager on duty did not know where my groceries were, but he did tell me to go pick out the groceries I had bought, and they would not charge me. As I sheepishly headed down the produce aisle, Ana, perched in the grocery cart, said, with her bright eyes, wide smile, and splayed arms, "What happened to the groceries? What happened to the groceries? What happened to the groceries?" Suddenly, the manager's voice came over the loudspeaker, "Will the man who lost his groceries please come to the help desk?" I felt like exulting, "Yes, that's me. I'm the one who lost his groceries." Instead, though, I simply pushed my cart, with downcast countenance and chipper daughter, to the help desk. There the manager told me that a staffer had seen my groceries languishing on the curb and put them in the refrigerator compartment in the back of the store. That was "what happened to the groceries." I put them in our car, and happily we all went home.

So, what's your story? How have you come to read this book? Perhaps you are a student in a course on the Bible. How did you come to be enrolled in this school rather than another one? How did you come to take this course? What are some favorite personal stories that have happened to you? What are some favorite family stories that are told over and over?

Stories are entertaining, exciting, suspenseful, and wonderful.

A Love Story

I said at the beginning that I wanted to tell you a story. Here is the one I had in mind when I said that. It is about how I fell in love . . . with biblical criticism.

I grew up Southern Baptist. I felt that God called me to ministry, so I went to school at "The" Southern Baptist Theological Seminary in Louisville, Kentucky. (Six Southern Baptist seminaries exist, but the one in Louisville was the oldest and, I thought, the best.) I had been a religion major at William Jewell College in Liberty, Missouri. In college I had tasted from the well of biblical criticism, but I did not know how deep this well was, how satisfying the water would be, or how much it would quench my thirst. As a Master of Divinity student I learned the historical criticism of the Bible, which was primarily what biblical criticism was in those days in the late 1970s and early 1980s. Specifically, I learned source, form, and redaction criticism.[2] In New Testament studies these critical methods were focused on the first three gospels, Matthew, Mark, and Luke, which are referred to as the "Synoptic gospels." (The word "synoptic" literally means "see together," which is taken in one of two senses. First, these three gospels see Jesus together, that is, they tell many of the stories in much the same order with much the same vocabulary. Second, because of these similarities you can set many of the stories side by side and "see them together." Indeed, a book that does just that is called a "synopsis," which is a very helpful tool for studying the Synoptic gospels.) Source criticism focused on the sources behind the Synoptic gospels. I learned that most scholars think that Mark was the first gospel written and that Matthew and Luke used it in composing their gospels. They also used a sayings source that is dubbed "Q," from the German word *Quelle,* which means "source." (Examples of sayings probably in Q include the Beatitudes, Matt 5:3-12; Luke 6:20-23; and the Lord's Prayer, Matt 6:9-15; Luke 11:2-4. Mark does not have either of these.) Form criticism focused on the various forms that stories and sayings took in teaching and preaching of the early church after Jesus' death in 30 and before the writing of Mark in 70. For example, the early Christian teachers and preachers told miracle stories, parables, controversy stories, and others, and each form had a particular purpose in the early church.

The "critical criticism" for me, though, was redaction criticism. It built on source criticism because it was concerned how the Synoptic Gospel writers (the "evangelists") "redacted," or adapted, their sources. For example, how did Luke redact Mark's story of the baptism (Luke 3:21-22; Mark 1:9-11)? Redaction critics maintained that Luke added the reference that Jesus was praying after being baptized and before receiving the Holy Spirit. Prayer is an important activity for Jesus in Luke; not only does he pray before receiving the Spirit, he also prays before choosing disciples (6:12), before being transfigured (9:29), and before giving the Lord's Prayer (11:1). Luke's Jesus is a praying man! He is also a Spirit-filled man. While Mark simply has "the Spirit descending," Luke says that "the Holy

---

[2] For further details see Catherine M. Murphy, *John the Baptist: Prophet of Purity for a New Age.* Interfaces (Collegeville: Liturgical Press, 2003).

Spirit descended upon him in bodily form." A little later, Luke says that Jesus came into Galilee "filled with the power of the Spirit" (4:14), and further along in the gospel he notes that "Jesus rejoiced in the Holy Spirit" (10:21). Furthermore, Luke appends to his gospel a second volume, which we know as the Acts of the Apostles, and in this volume Luke often notes that the Spirit led believers to do certain things. Jesus is Spirit-filled, and so are his followers!

I found all this fascinating. I became impressed with the evangelists' theological and pastoral skills. Redaction critics maintained that each evangelist crafted together his sources to form a document that spoke to the specific situations his community was experiencing. The evangelists did not write their gospels for the wider public, but rather for a specific network of churches they were part of. So in Synoptic studies there is much talk of the Matthean community and Markan theology. One of the reasons often advanced for the differences in the gospels is that they are addressed to different Christian communities in different situations. Why does Luke emphasize prayer and the Spirit? Because Luke's community was composed of Gentiles, and it was the prayerful and Spirit-filled Jesus and his prayerful and Spirit-filled disciples who brought the gospel to the Gentiles. Frequent mention of prayer and the Spirit legitimates the Gentiles' (and thus Luke's community's) place in the divine plan. Why does Mark emphasize Jesus' suffering? Because his community was suffering, either during or immediately after the first Jewish revolt against Rome, which ended with the destruction of the Jerusalem temple in 70. Markan Christians are encouraged to remain faithful in suffering because Jesus himself was faithful in his suffering. Matthew's Jesus teaches about righteousness "greater than the Pharisees'" (5:20) and sends disciples initially only to Jews (10:5-6), but after the resurrection he sends them to "all nations," that is, the Gentiles (28:20). It can be deduced, then, that Matthew's community was feeling increasingly alienated from Pharisaic Judaism and that these Christian Jews, who made up Matthew's community, were involved in evangelizing Gentiles.

I found redaction criticism so fascinating because I saw its potential for preaching and teaching in the contemporary church. If the gospels were addressed to circumstances in first-century churches, then they also could address circumstances in the twentieth-century church. I was a Baptist minister, looking perhaps to serve in the future as pastor of a Southern Baptist church, and redaction criticism fit into these vocational interests. Redaction criticism helped me bridge the gap between "then" and "now," between the ancient text and the contemporary setting.

Having fallen head over heels in love with biblical criticism while a Master of Divinity student, I went on to pursue my love interest as a Ph.D.

student, also at The Southern Baptist Seminary. During my first semester in the program I took a seminar on the Gospel of John with R. Alan Culpepper, who was just back from sabbatical in Cambridge, England. I had taken Culpepper for masters' level courses in Mark and in John, and I knew his approach, or at least I thought I did. Boy, was I in for a surprise! I noticed that first day in seminar that his sabbatical across the big water had changed Culpepper somehow. And it was to change me too. We looked at the gospel not as history but as *story*, that is, with plot, setting, and character. In other words, we looked at the Gospel of John the same way literary scholars looked at contemporary novels.

We learned all this from Culpepper's lectures and a rough draft he had written on sabbatical, a book published as *Anatomy of the Fourth Gospel: A Study in Literary Design*.[3] In this book he pursued what would later be called narrative criticism and reader-response criticism on the Gospel of John. Our other text, aside from the gospel itself, was not a book of biblical criticism, but one of literary criticism, Seymour Chatman, *Story and Discourse: Narrative Structure in Fiction and Film*.[4] Fiction and film?! What does that have to do with the Gospel of John? Much in every way, I found out. A gospel fundamentally is a story about Jesus. And as a story it has plot, it has setting, and it has characters. It was this last element that particularly attracted me. So I wrote a seminar paper on the characterization of Jesus and the Father in the Fourth Gospel. Characterization has always attracted me. My paper began this way:

> When we think of the stories we have read, we remember most vividly not the plot or the setting but the character around which the story revolves. We remember the miserly Ebenezer Scrooge, the mischievous Huck Finn, and the clever Sherlock Holmes. The main characters of the story come into our living rooms and stay awhile, long after other elements have gone.
>
> This is no less true in the Gospel of John. Through the eyes of the evangelist, we are confronted with the person of Jesus of Nazareth. . . .

As I read those words more than a score of years after I wrote them, I think my observation is still true. Characters emblazon themselves on our consciousness. I certainly feel that way about the Jesus of the Gospel of John and about the Gerasene demoniac of the Gospel of Mark.

---

[3] R. Alan Culpepper, *Anatomy of the Fourth Gospel: A Study in Literary Design*. Foundations & Facets: New Testament (Philadelphia: Fortress, 1983).

[4] Seymour Chatman, *Story and Discourse: Narrative Structure in Fiction and Film* (Ithaca, NY: Cornell University Press, 1978).

My paper ended, "Literary criticism opens up new vistas for the reading of the Gospel of John." (What I was referring to as "literary criticism" has now been dubbed in New Testament studies "narrative criticism.") My statement was true for me then, not only about John but also about all the gospels and Acts. And the statement holds true for me now. Indeed, I gathered insights in that seminar that I'm still unpacking over twenty years later. Narrative criticism has helped me in my teaching, writing, speaking, and preaching. It has enabled me to get a sense of the whole story, the whole gospel narrative. Source, form, and redaction criticism can be atomistic; that is, they can be focused on one small section of a gospel to the exclusion of the rest of the story (though redaction criticism can also look at a whole gospel, too). Narrative criticism also helped me get a sense of the story as contemporary readers read it. Historical criticism is so, well, "historical"—that is, it is often locked in the past. It is concerned for what lies behind the text rather than what lies on the surface of the text. A helpful image Culpepper used was that of the window and the mirror. If we see the text as window, then what is important is what is on the other side of the text. We are not interested in the text as such, but only as it serves to let us see what is behind it. If we see the text as mirror, however, then what is important is what is on the surface. We are interested in the text as such and what is shows us. Culpepper writes in the published form of his book: "The text is therefore a mirror in which readers can 'see' the world in which they live. Its meaning is produced in the experience of reading the gospel and lies on this side of the text, between the reader and the text."[5]

Learning to Love Mark's Story

I soon found out that we were in the middle of a major methodological shift in gospel studies. In the New Testament graduate colloquium we read two important books that took a narrative approach to Mark: *Mark's Story of Jesus* by Werner Kelber, and *Mark as Story: An Introduction to the Narrative of a Gospel* by David Rhoads and Donald Michie.[6] I take the Kelber volume off the shelf now, and as I thumb through it I am amazed at how much it has influenced my view of Mark. In a brief book written for a general audience Kelber lays bare the story line of the gospel, in which he views Mark as "a dramatically plotted journey of Jesus."[7] The Rhoads and

[5] Culpepper, *Anatomy,* 5.
[6] Werner Kelber, *Mark's Story of Jesus* (Philadelphia: Fortress, 1979); David Rhoads and Donald Michie, *Mark as Story: An Introduction to the Narrative of a Gospel* (Philadelphia: Fortress, 1982).
[7] Kelber, *Mark's Story,* 9.

Michie volume is written jointly by a religion professor and English professor at the same college, out of a course they team-taught. It was very similar to Culpepper's work, for they applied to Mark the categories Chatman had used in *Story and Discourse,* just as Culpepper had applied them to John.

I realized that scholars began to turn to narrative criticism in the mid-1970s out of some dissatisfaction with historical criticism. Biblical scholars had garnered much benefit from historical criticism. They had discovered that the text was "other." It was different from modern texts. Nevertheless, historical criticism had alienated Scripture from people. There was a great gulf fixed. How do we span that chasm?

Through story, some biblical scholars began to answer. College Bible professors began to talk to their colleagues not only in the history department but also in the literature department. They began to learn much from the study of modern fiction, especially the "New Criticism," which was very popular among students of English literature in the mid-20th century. "New Criticism" emphasized the work itself. It neglected the study of the historical background. Biblical critics, then, attempted to focus on the gospel stories themselves, not the history behind the stories. How did the story work? How did it get across its message? They decided to use the tools that literary critics were using on modern novels. They began to speak about plot, character and setting. They began to talk less about the ancient author and more about the implied author and the narrator.

As a result of these forays into the "New Criticism," New Testament scholars began to emphasize the whole story, not just slices of it. Each passage or episode was to be interpreted in the context of the rest of the story. "Context," then, came to mean not historical context, in which a passage was understood against the backdrop of a hypothetical community situation. Rather, "context" came to mean the narrative context. How does this episode contribute to the overall story? How does it move the reader along? So the critics focused on narrative. The gospels were narratives; they were stories. So the name "narrative criticism" grew up in biblical studies. There was actually no such thing in the study of literature. Narrative criticism referred to interpreting the gospels and Acts as narratives.

Narrative critics not only spoke about the whole story; they also spoke about the unity, or coherence, of the story. They looked at how the episodes of a gospel fit together into a coherent narrative. By contrast, historical biblical critics, especially source critics, would focus on the disjunctions in the document, that is, how certain sections do not fit with each other. They maintained that the disjunctions pointed to different sources that came out of communities in different situations in different times. For example, in

Mark we find two emphases: miracles and suffering. In roughly the first half of the gospel Jesus is going around performing miracles all over Galilee and the surrounding territory. He casts out demons, heals lepers, calms the sea, and walks on water. In the second half of the gospel, however, Jesus predicts his death and then goes to Jerusalem, where he is arrested, tried, and crucified. Historical critics have often said that Mark has inherited two sources: a Passion narrative, which tells of Jesus' arrest, trial, death, and burial, and a cycle of miracle stories. Mark has combined the two sources, emphasizing the suffering, principally by inserting a number of times when Jesus silences people who are healed. Critics have called this theme the "messianic secret." We will say more about this later, in the next chapter.[8]

Narrative critics approach it differently. They do not deny the possibility of the scenario the historical critics have mapped out, but their focus is elsewhere. Rather than looking for layers of tradition, they look at how everything fits together in one coherent story. Mark the evangelist, they maintain, was not just a scissors-and-paste person snipping and gluing together various pieces of tradition from various sources, as form critics have it; he was an author who wrote a story. Narrative critics do not attempt to divide the gospel into layers of tradition, but rather to discover the unity the story contains. They do not ask: What source does this passage belong to, and what source does that passage belong to? Instead, they ask: How do this episode and that episode contribute to the overall story? In Mark's case, how do the miracles and the suffering fit together in the narrative? How do Jesus' instructions to silence contribute to the bringing together of these two themes in one narrative?

Mark, for various reasons, was the first gospel to which narrative criticism was applied. First, it was likely the first gospel written. Second, it is the shortest, with only sixteen chapters, while Matthew has twenty-eight, Luke twenty-four, and John twenty-one. Finally, it was the gospel that had had the least attention paid it throughout Christian history. Sandwiched between Matthew and Luke, Mark was the "Rodney Dangerfield" of the gospels, for it "got no respect." Biblical critics, however, are always looking for ideas, fragments, documents, or groups that have been long ignored or overlooked. Mark has been overshadowed by the three other gospels, so it was time to bring it out into the spotlight.

Chatman Making a Mark

How, then, did narrative biblical critics lure Mark out into the spotlight? Seymour Chatman has proven most helpful and influential. In the

---

[8] See below, Chapter 2, 22.

schema he describes in *Story and Discourse* he makes a distinction between the "real world" and "the world of the text." In the real world are the "real" authors and the "real" reader. The real author is the flesh-and-blood person who actually puts pen to paper (or fingers to computer keyboard!) to create a document, such as the one we call the Gospel of Mark. It seems that the title "The Gospel of Mark" was placed on the book when the gospels were collected together, perhaps seventy years or so after they were written. The title was based on a tradition that the book was written by John Mark, a disciple of Peter in Rome. But the book itself does not say that. Originally this gospel, like the other three, was anonymous; the text itself does not give the name of its "real author."

Just as real, flesh-and-blood authors write texts, so real, flesh-and-blood readers read them. Real readers read the Gospel of Mark in the first century, and they have continued to do so into the twenty-first century. When I pick up a copy of the Gospel of Mark, I am a real reader, and when you pick it up, you are a real reader. Really! Read on!

In the real world are the real author and the real reader. In the text, however, are the "implied" author and the "implied" reader. The author and the reader in the text are "implied" in that the text "implies," rather than explicitly states, who these people are. The implied author, then, is the sum of what we can know about the author from the text itself. We surmise that the implied author of the Gospel of Mark is a Greek-speaking first-century Mediterranean Christian: "Greek-speaking" because the document was originally written in Greek, "first-century Mediterranean" because the gospel tells about people and events that happened in that time and place, and "Christian" because Jesus is said to be the Christ and the Son of God. We might distinguish between implied author and real author in that the real author of the Gospel of Mark is dead, but the implied author still lives on when we read the text.

Also living on in the text is the implied reader. The implied reader, however, is the reader for whom the document is written. (Sometimes critics speak about the "ideal reader.") The implied author is trying to move the implied reader to feel, think, and do certain things. The implied reader is a creation of the text, as the implied author is. If there is no text, there is no implied author or implied reader. In Mark the implied reader would probably be described in much the same way as the implied author: a Greek-speaking first-century Mediterranean Christian. The same reasons hold for the implied reader. The reader has to speak Greek in order to understand the work, and it seems likely that the reader is living in the same time and place as the author. Does the implied author imagine that the reader is already a Christian before reading the document? This is a good question. Another way to frame it is to say: Was this book written to evangelize nonbelievers or to teach believers? (Mark does not have a purpose statement as John has in John 20:31: "But these things are written so that you might believe that the Christ, the Son of God, is Jesus, and that as you believe in his name, you might have life." Unfortunately, this statement does not really clarify the purpose of the gospel because it is unclear whether "believe" means "begin to believe" or "continue to believe.") It seems that Mark and the other gospels were in-house documents, meant for teaching believers. Ultimately, though, a decision on that point is not crucial for interpretation. The implied author certainly assumes that the implied reader will be a Christian by the end of the document, if not at the beginning.

It is worth noting here that we twenty-first-century English-speaking North Americans are NOT the implied readers of the Gospel of Mark, or of any books of the New Testament. They were written for first-century Greek-speaking Mediterraneans. In some ways we are "overhearing" a conversation from long ago. To change the image, we are reading someone else's mail. The text is still "other," as historical biblical criticism taught us, and we do injustice to the text if we treat it as if it were written by and for twenty-first-century English-speaking North Americans. We must respect the distance rather than collapse it. It is at this point that historical criticism and narrative criticism go hand in hand. It is important that we understand as much as we can about first-century Greek-speaking Mediterraneans so that we might understand the shared values, assumptions, and worldviews of the implied (and real) author and readers.

In many ways, implied "reader" is anachronistic for the first-century Mediterranean world. The Gospel of Mark, like all the New Testament documents, was written to be read aloud. People would not have had personal copies of the gospel that they read silently in the privacy of their homes. Believers would have gathered together to hear the gospel read aloud. Literacy was low, and the price of writing materials was high. Furthermore, reading was difficult, as first-century Christian documents did not have punctuation, capitalization, or even spaces between the words!

In the text are not only the implied author and reader, but also the narrator and narratee. The narrator tells the story to the narratee. In modern fiction the narrator and narratee may be characters in the narrative. In the Gospel of Mark, as well as the other gospels, the narrator is not a character in the story.[9] Indeed, the narrator in the Gospel of Mark is omniscient and

---

[9] Luke and Acts, which are two volumes by the same author, have a unique twist on the narrator and narratee. At the beginning of both Luke and Acts the story is told to someone

omnipresent. In other words, the narrator is all-seeing, telling readers what characters are thinking and feeling. The narrator is also all-present, going not only where Jesus goes, but also to places where Jesus does not go, such as the dwelling places of the Gerasene demoniac (Mark 5:3-5) and the courts of Herod Antipas, ruler of Galilee (6:14-29). In Mark's case, then, the implied author and the narrator are identical, as are the implied reader and the narratee. (In this book I will refer to the implied author, or narrator, as "Mark," though the author nowhere in the document gives a name. I will also refer to the implied readers, or narratees, as "we" or "us." I do so reservedly because of the comments I made above. Yet as we read Mark's story we are the "real readers," and the idea that Mark is communicating directly to "us" does give some immediacy to the story.)

Plotting the Gospels

The narrator tells a story to the narratee. This story has plot, setting, and character. Plot is what happens and why it happens. Setting is where it happens, and character is who makes it happen or who it happens to. The gospels (including John) have similar plots, settings, and characters, yet they are different. In my Introduction to New Testament I class, which covers the gospels and Acts, I have the following plot statements for each gospel:

> **Mark:** Jesus the Son of God works miracles, teaches, and calls disciples, yet in doing so he meets opposition, which leads to his being rejected and killed, but God raises him.

> **Matthew:** Jesus, Son of God from conception, teaches about the reign of the heavens, works miracles, and calls disciples; however, he meets opposition, ultimately suffering rejection and crucifixion, but he triumphs through resurrection to be with the disciples to the end of the age.

> **Luke:** Jesus, Son of God from conception, fulfills Scripture by healing, teaching, and calling all people (especially outcasts) and by dying, rising, and sending his disciples out to proclaim.

---

named Theophilus (Luke 1:1-4; Acts 1:1-2), so that he becomes the narratee. Acts also has a narrator who very occasionally becomes a character. In the second half of the book the pronoun "we" appears in a few sections. For example, "we" cross over to the Greek province of Macedonia and go to a city of Philippi (16:10-17), and "we" experience a frightful storm and shipwreck while sailing on the Mediterranean Sea (27:1–28:16; see also 20:5-15; 21:1-18). It is difficult to know how to interpret these "we" references, which are comparatively sparse in this long document of Acts.

John: Jesus the eternal Son comes down from above in order to reveal the Father through miraculous signs, self-referring discourses, and ultimately death, resurrection, and ascension, in which he returns to the Father and sends the Spirit.

Whenever I read over these plot statements I am reminded of one of the favorite books of my younger daughter Miranda, *Cherry Pies and Lullabies*.[10] Through four generations, a mother makes a pie, a quilt, and a crown of flowers for her daughter. After each gift the narrator, who is a character in the story, has the refrain: "Every time it was the same but different." Miranda always asks, "How is it the same but different?" and then she tells me. These plot statements of the four gospels are "the same but different." How are they the same but different? They are the same because they all speak of the same main character, Jesus, who does much the same things, such as miracles, teaching, and death and resurrection. They are different because of the way each gospel puts these activities together in a coherent narrative. For example, compare the first several words of each plot statement. Mark's statement begins, "Jesus the Son of God," while Matthew's and Luke's statements each begin, "Jesus, Son of God from conception." Mark tells nothing about Jesus prior to his adulthood. He comes to John for baptism "all grown-up" (see Mark 1:9). Matthew and Luke, however, both tell of Jesus' special conception and birth, though they tell it from different perspectives and narrate different events. For example, in Matthew the angel appears to Joseph (in a dream), while in Luke the angel appears to Mary (while she is awake!); in Matthew the wise men come to Jesus, and in Luke the shepherds visit (see Matt 1:18–2:12; Luke 1:26-38; 2:8-20). (The nativity scenes that have both shepherds and wise men are a conflation of Matthew and Luke!) Nevertheless, both Matthew and Luke depict Jesus as Son of God and savior from his conception, while Mark begins his story of the Son of God with the baptism.

John, however, goes back even farther. Jesus in John is the eternal Son. "In the beginning was the word. . . . And the word became flesh" (John 1:1, 14). The word-in-the-beginning becomes flesh in Jesus of Nazareth. John begins the story with the beginning, Matthew and Luke with Jesus' conception and birth, and Mark with his baptism.

Notice also what Jesus does in these gospels. Again, what he does is the same but different. In all four gospels Jesus works miracles and teaches, but in each these activities are given different emphases and different contexts. In Mark, Jesus' exorcisms and healings take up proportion-

---

[10] Lynn Reiser, *Cherry Pies and Lullabies* (New York: Greenwillow Books, 1998).

ally more of the narrative than in the other gospels. In Matthew, Jesus is certainly a miracle-worker, but he is primarily a teacher, delivering five "lectures" to his pupils the disciples. In Luke, Jesus heals and teaches, but he does these so that the Scripture might be fulfilled (4:14-21). In John, Jesus works wonders and teaches, but he does so as one who has come down from above, so that his wonders are referred to as "signs" and his discourses refer to himself ("I am the bread of life," . . .) rather than to the reign of God or the reign of the heavens, as in the Synoptics.

The settings in the gospels are also the same but different. They all take place in what is now known as the Middle East, in Galilee and Jerusalem. Mark sets forth the basic story line: Jesus is active in Galilee, with brief forays outside the region, such as into Gerasa in our episode. He is particularly active around the lake known as the Sea of Galilee. After a time in Galilee, he then goes to Jerusalem (about fifty miles south of Galilee), where he is killed by the Jewish and Roman authorities and is raised by God. Matthew takes these same settings and expands them. Jesus first appears in Bethlehem, near Jerusalem, and escapes the evil King Herod by going to Egypt in Africa. He then settles in Galilee, where he ministers as an adult, and then he travels to Jerusalem, the site of his death and resurrection, after which he returns to Galilee to meet the disciples. Luke begins in Jerusalem (with John the Baptist's parents, Zechariah and Elizabeth), moves back to Galilee (with Mary), moves south to Bethlehem for Jesus' birth, back to Galilee for Jesus' growing up, goes to Jerusalem for Jesus' trip to the Temple at age twelve, back to Galilee, where Jesus grows up and is active as an adult, then to Jerusalem (taking up much of the narrative getting there), where he dies, is raised, and appears in the area. John begins in the world above, with the Word and God. Jesus comes down "from above," and makes three trips from Galilee to Jerusalem and back. On his fourth trip to Jerusalem he dies and rises, which is the way he returns to God.

The Character(s) of the Gospels

In all four gospels Jesus is the main character, and the disciples constitute a major character group. At times in the Synoptics Peter, James, and John have narrative roles apart from the rest of the disciples. In Mark the disciples consistently misunderstand, and they forsake Jesus when he is arrested. In Matthew they come off a little better, as they are "ones of little faith," though they still forsake Jesus at his arrest, though they do see Jesus in Galilee, where they are entrusted with the commission to evangelize. In Luke the disciples "are kept" from understanding, but their eyes and minds are opened when Jesus appears to them (thus setting up their going out to evangelize in Acts). In John the disciples do not function as a group in the same way as in the Synoptics. Individuals stand out, especially Peter and the anonymous "disciple whom Jesus loved," but also Nathanael, Thomas, Andrew, and Philip.

The disciples are not the only character group; in the Synoptics the other major group are the Pharisees (who are sometimes combined with the scribes for that dastardly duo "scribes and Pharisees"). They are consistently portrayed as the villains to Jesus the hero, antagonists to Jesus the protagonist. They continually harass Jesus and his disciples while he is in Galilee. In Matthew, Jesus is particularly harsh in his criticism of them, pronouncing "woes" upon them and calling them "whitewashed tombs" and "a brood of vipers" (Matt 23:13-36).

The Pharisees appear in John, but the character group most often opposed to Jesus is a group known as the "Judeans" (called "Jews" in most translations). Sometimes the name for this group is alternately "Judeans" and "Pharisees." In John, therefore, it is Jesus against the Judeans.

The major characters include Jesus, the disciples, and the Pharisees (or in John, the Judeans). A host of minor characters, however, fill out the narratives of the gospels. In Mark they include our friend the Gerasene along with the Syro-Phoenician woman, Bartimaeus, and the woman who anointed Jesus (5:1-20; 7:24-30; 10:46-52; 14:3-9). All of these are presented in a positive light. The first three mentioned all receive a miracle from Jesus, and the fourth responds in a faithful manner. Not all minor characters are depicted so positively. A young man who asks Jesus about eternal life does not follow him because he is rich (10:17-22). He resembles the disciples, who begin promisingly but end in failure. Then there is the Roman governor Pontius Pilate, who condemns Jesus to death (15:1-15). He resembles the Pharisees as a consistent opponent of Jesus.

Matthew and Luke have many of these same characters, though Matthew doubles the Gerasene and then moves the pair closer to the sea of Galilee, so that the two demoniacs are Gadarenes (Matt 8:28-34). Similarly, Matthew doubles the blind man Mark names as Bartimaeus (20:29-34). Furthermore, Matthew calls the Syro-Phoenician a "Canaanite" (15:21-28), and Luke omits her altogether. Both Matthew and Luke tell about the woman who anoints Jesus, but in Matthew as in Mark she anoints Jesus in preparation for his death near the end of the story (26:6-13), while in Luke she anoints Jesus about a third of the way through the story as a sign of her great love for Jesus (Luke 7:36-50).

Because Matthew and Luke have more material than Mark, they have a few more characters. The opening sections of both gospels, which tell of

Jesus' conception and birth, are illustrative (see Matthew 1–2; Luke 1–2). Of course, both have Mary and Joseph, with Matthew giving more attention to Joseph and Luke focusing more on Mary. Matthew tells of the wise men from the East who come to worship the baby Jesus and the evil king Herod who tries to kill him. Luke features exclusively righteous characters, including Zechariah and Elizabeth, who are John the Baptist's aged parents, and Simeon and Anna, who acclaim the baby Jesus in the Temple.

Again, John is different. Characters appear here who do not appear elsewhere in the gospels. We see Nicodemus, who comes to Jesus by night (John 3:1-21), and the Samaritan woman, who discusses true worship with Jesus at the well (4:7-42). The paralytic by the pool of Bethzatha and the man born blind are both healed by Jesus (5:1-18), as is his beloved Lazarus (11:1-44), whose sisters Mary and Martha are also beloved and also appear in Luke (Luke 10:38-42). Similarly, Mary Magdalene also appears in the Synoptics, but in John she is accorded the first appearance of Jesus after his resurrection (John 20:1-18).

Conclusion

Such are the kinds of observations that narrative critics make. They realize the importance of story to the human condition, and they highlight the gospels as story. Furthermore, they emphasize the whole story each gospel tells and the unity of that story. Seymour Chatman's schema of real and implied author and reader has proven helpful, as has analyzing a gospel story's plot, setting, and character.

I hope you have picked up some of my enthusiasm for narrative criticism, an enthusiasm that goes back over twenty years. I hope you can better appreciate the gospels' narrative qualities and that this way of looking gives you a new understanding of the gospels. What do you think?

In the next chapter we will consider the Gospel of Mark alone, so that we can better understand the narrative context in which the Gerasene appears. (The "g" is a hard "g" as in "gas." "Gerasene" rhymes with "wear-a-scene.") Let us travel with Mark on his journey as he tells us the story of Jesus.

CHAPTER TWO

Mark My Word:
The Story of the Crucified Son of God

Let me tell you another story.

This story, though, is not a story that happened to me. It is not a story in which I am a character. No, it is Mark's story. As I say in the title for this chapter, it is the story of the crucified Son of God. All the gospels tell about Jesus' crucifixion, but none seems to place it as centrally as does Mark. The first thing I want to do in this chapter is to trace Mark's story line. Because narrative critics emphasize the whole story, I want you to have a sense of the whole story of the Gospel of Mark. I want to review the plot statement I gave for Mark in the previous chapter and unpack it a little more. I want to give particular attention to the section of the story in which our episode about the Gerasene appears.

First, though, have you read the gospel straight through in one sitting? If not, STOP. Do not pass GO; do not collect $200; go directly to a Bible (I prefer the New Revised Standard Version) and read it from beginning to end at one time. After you have done that, you may continue in this book.

What follows is my summary of the plot. I particularly focus on repetitions, patterns, and allusions. Perhaps I point out some things that you didn't see as you read. And maybe you saw some things that I don't point out. If so, great! Compare your reading of Mark with mine.

Here is the plot statement I gave for Mark in the last chapter:

> Jesus the Son of God works miracles, teaches, and calls disciples, yet in doing so he meets opposition, which leads to his being rejected and killed, but God raises him.

I want to use this statement as a framework to tell Mark's story. Ancient stories are plot-driven, while modern stories seem more character-driven, so it seems appropriate to approach this ancient story through plot. We will take each element of the statement and discuss what Mark says about it.

"Jesus the Son of God . . ."

Jesus is the main character of Mark's story, and he is Son of God. Mark says that in the very first line of his story: "The beginning of the gospel of Jesus Christ, Son of God."[1] For Mark, Jesus was not an ordinary human being; he was Christ, which means the same thing as "Messiah." "Christ" comes from the Greek and "Messiah" comes from the Hebrew, and both mean "anointed one." Jesus was not only Christ but also "Son of God." Here Mark states his "evaluative point of view." He comes at the story from a decidedly Christian stance. His main character Jesus is not just Jesus the prophet or Jesus of Nazareth, but "Jesus Christ, Son of God." Of these two names, Mark's favorite is "Son of God." Indeed, in one of the opening episodes of the story God confirms what Mark has already said, that Jesus is God's son (Mark 1:9). When Jesus is coming up out of the water from his baptism, he sees the heavens ripping open and the Spirit coming down into him, and a voice comes out of the heavens: "You are my son, the beloved, in you I delight." Perhaps we recognize that this voice seems to be echoing three statements from the Hebrew Scriptures: Genesis 22:2, Psalm 2:7, and Isaiah 42:1, all of which feature God speaking. (It seems that Mark expects that we, his readers, will have a thorough knowledge of the Hebrew Scriptures.) In Ps 2:7 God says to the newly inaugurated king, "You are my son; today I have begotten you." In Isa 42:1 God says (it is unclear to whom), "Here is my servant, whom I uphold, my chosen, in whom my soul delights; I have put my spirit upon him; he will bring forth justice to the nations." In Gen 22:2 God says to Abraham, "Take your son, your only son Isaac, whom you love, and go to the land of Moriah, and offer him there as a burnt offering on one of the mountains that I shall show you." Through these allusions to the Hebrew Scriptures Mark wants us to know that Jesus is the royal, Spirit-endowed, justice-producing, self-sacrificing Son of God.[2]

---

[1] The Bible you are reading may have a note that says that some manuscripts do not have "son of God." We actually do not have any original manuscripts; all we have are copies of copies of copies, and those copies do not all agree. While most manuscripts have "Jesus Christ, son of God," others simply have "Jesus Christ."

[2] All quotations from the New Testament are my own translations. All quotations from the Hebrew Scriptures are from the New Revised Standard Version.

God calls Jesus "beloved son" at the beginning of the story, when Jesus is baptized and empowered with the Spirit, and again right in the middle of the story, when Jesus is transfigured, along with Moses and Elijah (prominent figures in the Hebrew Scriptures). God says (apparently to Peter, James, and John, the disciples accompanying Jesus), "This is my son, the beloved, listen to him" (9:7). Listen to him say what? That Jesus is going to die and be raised, and that his followers must deny themselves, take up their cross, and follow him (8:31, 34). This Jesus Son of God, then, is going to die, and his followers must also be prepared to die!

So both Mark and God say that Jesus is God's son. But they are not the only ones. You may remember that our friend the Gerasene calls Jesus "son of the highest god." (The first man from whom Jesus exorcizes a demon calls Jesus a related title, "holy one of God.") Indeed, at the seaside Jesus casts out unclean spirits, who cry out that he is "Son of God" (3:11). (The term "unclean spirit" is a Jewish term, while "demon" is Greek, or Gentile.) Supernatural figures, then, acknowledge that Jesus is Son of God. Humans, however, do not recognize it. This is one of the ironies of the gospel: the demons recognize that Jesus is Son of God, but humans do not—not the religious authorities, and not even Jesus' disciples. Indeed, the disciples never say that Jesus is Son of God (at least in Mark; in Matthew, however, they do: see Matt 14:33). When Jesus asks the disciples who they say he is, Peter says that he is the Christ. (In Matthew, Peter also says that Jesus is "the Son of the living God," 16:16). Jesus, however, hushes Peter up, and goes on to tell about his suffering (Mark 8:29-31). Although Mark calls Jesus "Christ, Son of God," he is ambivalent about describing Jesus as "Christ" and prefers "Son of God."

". . . Works Miracles . . ."

As the Spirit-endowed Son of God, Jesus works miracles, as noted in my plot statement. Jesus is baptized and receives the Spirit; he overcomes temptation by Satan, and then he comes into Galilee preaching that the reign (or kingdom, as it is usually translated) of God is drawing near. Jesus' first public act, which demonstrates that the reign of God is drawing near, is to cast out an unclean spirit from a man in the synagogue in Capernaum (1:21-28). Exorcisms are very important activities for Mark and for his main character Jesus. Jesus does more exorcisms than any other kind of miracle. Mark tells us of four exorcisms: this one in the synagogue in Capernaum, the one of the Gerasene that is the focus of this book (5:1-20), the daughter of the Syrophoenician woman (7:24-30), and the deaf and mute boy brought by his father (9:14-29). Furthermore, three times Mark includes summaries of healing activities (1:32-33, 39; 3:7-12), and in each of these casting out of demons figures prominently. Most importantly, though, Jesus indicates that his exorcisms are a demonstration that he is binding the strong man Satan, entering his house, and plundering his property. He casts out demons not by the prince of demons, as the scribes charge; rather he exorcizes unclean spirits by the Holy Spirit. Failure to recognize this is eternal, unforgivable sin (3:22-30).

Jesus not only casts out demons; he also heals people from various afflictions. Right after Jesus casts the unclean spirit out of the man in the synagogue in Capernaum, he "immediately" goes to Simon and Andrew's house, where he relieves Simon's mother-in-law of a fever (1:29-31). The evening following the healing of Simon's mother-in-law, the townspeople come to Simon's house and bring to Jesus "all who were sick and who were demonized." He cured the sick and exorcized the demons (1:32-34). Then, on a preaching mission in Galilee, he cleanses a leper (1:40-45) and, returning to Capernaum, he heals a paralytic (2:1-12).

A few observations about these miracle stories "from Capernaum to Capernaum," that is, beginning with the exorcism in the synagogue and ending with the healing of the paralytic (1:21–2:12): First, notice the pace at which Mark tells the story. Things often happen "immediately." For example, when Jesus is at the synagogue in Capernaum, "immediately" a man with an unclean spirit appears (1:23). After that Jesus "immediately" goes into Simon and Andrew's house (1:29). Not long after, Jesus tells the leper to be clean, and "immediately" the leprosy leaves him and he is clean (1:41-42). This is not the first time we have seen that word. At his baptism Jesus comes up out of the water and "immediately" he sees the heavens ripped apart and the Spirit coming down (1:10). After he hears the voice, the Spirit "immediately" throws Jesus out into the desert to be tempted by Satan (1:12). When Jesus calls Simon and Andrew from their fishing nets, they "immediately" leave them (1:18). (Some translations have "just as" or "right after" or "immediately" or "suddenly," but all of these English words are translations of the same Greek word.) Mark's tempo is fast, especially in the first several episodes of the story. Jesus did this, and then he did this, immediately he did this, and suddenly this happened. A related element is that Mark often begins a sentence with the conjunction "and." Jesus did this and this and he did this and they did this and he said this. Mark moves us along quickly. He has a message to tell, and he must do so fast.

Another observation is that Jesus often silences those he heals. In the synagogue in Capernaum he rebukes the unclean spirit in the man and says, "Be quiet, and come out of him" (1:25). In casting out the demons at Simon's door he does not let the demons speak because they knew him

(1:34, presumably that he was Son of God, see 3:11-12). When Jesus cleanses the leper he tells him not to say anything to anyone, but the healed man "proclaimed it much," so much so that Jesus could not go into a city, but had to stay out in the country (1:43-45).

This particular phenomenon is typically called the "messianic secret." The term is not quite accurate, because only in one circumstance is it Jesus' identity as Messiah, or Christ, that is being kept a secret. Much ink has been spilled on (and trees sacrificed for!) this question, but mostly it has been done from a historical perspective: Why would Jesus have told people not to tell anyone about him? Various answers have been offered, but it is important to consider how this secrecy functions in the narrative. To put it simply, it seems that Mark plays down the significance of the miracles so as to play up another aspect of Jesus' activity, that is, his death. Mark's story is not primarily the story of the wonderworking Son of God. That is an aspect to it, but that is not all of it. His story is primarily that of the crucified Son of God. So one way Mark subordinates miracles to crucifixion is through the "messianic secret."

The final observation about this section of the narrative is that it is nicely bracketed with the exorcism in the synagogue on the one hand and the healing of the paralytic on the other. A number of key words or themes link these two episodes together. Both happen in Capernaum. Jesus first goes to Capernaum after calling the first disciples, he does a few more miracles in the city, then he embarks on a preaching mission in Galilee in which he heals a leper, and then he returns to Capernaum, where he heals this paralytic. Another prominent word in both episodes is "authority." Indeed, that word appears twice in the synagogue exorcism episode. People are astounded at his teaching because he is teaching as one with authority (1:22). Following the exorcism, folks say, "What is this? A new teaching—with authority!" (1:27). Jesus justifies his healing of the paralytic by saying, "So that you will know that the son of humanity has authority on earth to forgive sins, I say to you, get up, take up your bed and go home" (2:10-11). (It is interesting to note that although God, demons, and the narrator call Jesus "Son of God," Jesus refers to himself as "son of humanity," see also 2:28; 8:31; etc.)

Because of Jesus' authority people are amazed, both in the synagogue following the exorcism, where they are amazed at his new authoritative teaching that enables him to cast out unclean spirits (1:27), and at home following the healing of the paralytic. When the man takes up his bed and goes out, everyone is amazed and glorifies God, saying, "We've never seen anything like this!" (2:12).

Mark describes Jesus as an authoritative teacher, not like the scribes (1:22). This narrative statement sets up the conflict with Jesus and the scribes at Capernaum. Jesus says to the paralytic who has been lowered through the roof by his faithful companions, "Child, your sins are forgiven." The scribes, who, Mark has already stated, have less authority than Jesus, now appear. They "dialogue in their hearts" about what Jesus has said, and they accuse him of blasphemy. "Who can forgive sins but God alone?" Jesus spiritually knows what they are thinking and challenges them with the question, "What's easier? Saying to the paralytic, 'Your sins are forgiven,' or saying, 'Get up, take your bed and walk'?" Then as the son of humanity, who authoritatively forgives sin, he tells the man to take a hike, which he does (2:5-12). Such is the authority of the one who teaches, heals, and forgives in un-scribe-like fashion.

Incidentally, Mark is fond of bracketing stories the way he does with these miracles near the beginning of the narrative. Later on, in the middle of the story, two healings of blind men bracket Jesus' telling the disciples about his impending arrest, death, and resurrection (8:22–10:52). These brackets, or inclusions, can appear in sections of episodes and in episodes themselves. We saw in the episode about the synagogue exorcism in Capernaum that the story both begins and ends with references to Jesus' authoritative teaching (1:22, 27). This use of inclusions helps people remember as they hear (and read) the story.

The scribes continue to harass Jesus, though they are called "the scribes of the Pharisees" when they complain about Jesus eating dinner with tax collectors and sinners (2:16). This begins a series of stories in which Jesus is in controversy with the Pharisees. They question him about his disciples' not fasting (2:18-21) and their picking grain on the Sabbath (2:23-28), and they object to Jesus' healing on the Sabbath a man with a withered hand, so much so that they plot to kill Jesus! (3:1-6). As with the healing of the paralytic (2:1-12), Mark combines a healing and a controversy story. In both episodes he asks his opponents a question with two choices (see 2:9; 3:4). Then he accomplishes the miracle. At the house in Capernaum everyone is amazed and glorifies God (2:12), but here in the synagogue the Pharisees go out and conspire to kill Jesus! (3:6). Here, early in the narrative, Jesus' death casts a shadow over the whole story.

Jesus casts out demons and heals people of various afflictions. On one occasion he even brings a girl back to life. Soon after the exorcism of the Gerasene, Jesus returns to Galilee, where a synagogue leader named Jairus asks Jesus to heal his daughter. On the way, Jesus heals a woman with a hemorrhage. News arrives that Jairus' daughter has died, but Jesus goes to resuscitate her with the words in Aramaic (the language Jesus spoke): "Talitha cum," which means, "Little girl, I say to you, get up." The girl was twelve years old, just as the woman had been hemorrhaging for twelve years (5:21-42). This "sandwiching" of one story inside another, technically called "intercalation," is another favorite of Mark. He does it with Jesus' family coming to get him when they hear people think he is crazy, combined with the controversy with the Jerusalem scribes over the source of his power to cast out demons (3:19b-35). He also does it with the cursing and withering of the fig tree, which sandwiches the action in the Temple (11:12-25).

Jesus casts out demons, heals, and resuscitates. He also does "nature miracles," that is, he manipulates inanimate objects. The nature miracles include the cursing and withering of the fig tree just mentioned. Most of these miracles occur in the section just prior to the halfway point in the narrative, which includes the exorcism of the Gerasene. This section includes three sea crossings (4:35-41; 6:45-52; 8:14-21) and two feedings (6:30-43; 8:1-10). Two of the three sea crossings involve "nature miracles," calming the storm and walking on the water, and the third involves a conversation about the feedings. In the first of these Jesus feeds five thousand Galilean men (women and children are not counted) from five loaves of bread and two fish. In the second feeding, which happens on the other side of the Sea of Galilee, he feeds from seven loaves and a few fish at least four thousand people. (Mark at this point does not say that they were men.) It is interesting to note that Jesus performs many of the same miracles on both sides of the sea: he casts out an unclean spirit in a synagogue in Capernaum in Galilee (1:21-28), and he casts out a legion of demons in Gerasa in the Decapolis, or the Ten Cities (5:1-20). He resuscitates Jairus' daughter in Galilee (5:21-45), and from afar he casts a demon out of the Syrophoenician's daughter (7:24-30). He feeds five thousand with five loaves and two fish in Galilee (6:30-44), and he feeds four thousand with seven loaves and a few fish across in the Decapolis (8:1-10). Jesus spends most of his career in Jewish Galilee, but he also crosses the sea to Gentile territory. In his boat crossings and in his healings Jesus is bringing together Jew and Gentile.

". . . Teaches . . ."

Much of Jesus' teaching is combined with his miracles. The episode of the exorcism in the synagogue at Capernaum actually begins with Jesus teaching. Mark does not say exactly what he was teaching. A little earlier Mark says that Jesus came into Galilee proclaiming, "The time is fulfilled, and the reign of God has drawn near; repent and believe in the gospel" (1:14-15). Apparently, then, Jesus is teaching about the drawing-near reign of God. It is this teaching that is astonishingly authoritative, and when

Jesus combines it with an exorcism the onlookers are amazed at Jesus' authoritatively new teaching, which commands obedience even from unclean spirits!

In these several opening episodes of the narrative most of Jesus' teaching is done in controversy with the scribes and Pharisees, often involving his miracles and other behavior, either his own or his disciples'. Only with his speech full of parables (4:1-34) does Mark include a block of Jesus' teachings. It begins with the parable of the sower, which Jesus interprets for the Twelve, the parable of the growing seed, and the parable of the mustard seed. Jesus explicitly compares the second and third parables with "the reign of God." (We can assume that the reign of God is also the subject of the first parable.) Twice it is noted, first by Jesus and then by Mark, that Jesus speaks to the crowd only through parables, but he explains everything to the disciples in private. To them is given the mystery of the reign of God. They are insiders, while the crowd constitutes the outsiders. Indeed, Jesus tells the crowd parables so that they will not understand (4:12, quoting from Isa 6:9-10)! This is strange teaching if the teacher does not want the hearers to understand!

Jesus' next major speech comes in response to the scribes' and Pharisees' questions about the disciples eating without washing their hands according to the "tradition of the elders," which the Pharisees observe (Mark 7:5). (Mark adds a narrative aside in 7:34 so that we can understand that the Pharisees wash hands, food, and cooking utensils before eating. He often uses narrative asides, as we saw when he translated the Aramaic Jesus spoke to the dead girl in 5:41; he translates another Aramaic word in this speech at 7:11.) Jesus begins his criticism of the Pharisees and scribes with a quotation from the prophet Isaiah, just as Mark began his narrative with Isaiah (1:2-3, though the first two lines of quotation are not from Isaiah, but probably from two other books in the Hebrew Scriptures, Malachi and Exodus; the fourth, fifth, and sixth lines, however, are from Isa 40:3). Jesus accuses them of abandoning God's commandment in favor of human tradition. He then quotes from the Ten Commandments, specifically the commandment to honor one's parents (Exod 20:12), along with a related statement in Deuteronomy (5:16), and says that a practice of the Pharisees effectively voids God's word.

Jesus then widens the audience by calling the crowd and telling them that what makes a person ritually impure is what comes out of a person, not what goes in. Jesus then goes into a house with his insiders, the disciples, and they ask him "about the parable," just as they did in his first speech (Mark 4:10). He says that what goes into a person enters the belly, not the heart, and that "evil intentions" come from within and make someone ritually impure.

Mark adds another narrative aside, saying that with these statements Jesus "cleansed all food" (7:19). With this teaching Mark prepares us for Jesus' encounter with the Syrophoenician woman, whom Mark notes is a Gentile (7:24-30). No distinction is to be made between pure and impure, children and dogs, Jews and Gentiles. Purity questions will arise in the next chapter when we focus on the Gerasene.

The final major block of Jesus' teaching occurs about three-fourths of the way through the narrative when Jesus answers the question of his disciples about the destruction of the Jerusalem Temple (13:1-37). Jesus predicts false messiahs and prophets, wars, earthquakes, famines, and "the desolating sacrilege," to which Mark adds another narrative aside, "Let the reader understand." (We don't!) These catastrophes will culminate in a cosmic crisis, in which the sun and moon will grow dark and the stars will fall (echoing words from the Hebrew prophets Isaiah, Ezekiel, and Joel). Then the son of humanity will come on the clouds (seemingly a quotation from the Hebrew prophet Daniel, 7:13) in order to gather the elect. Jesus says that he does not know when these things are going to take place, and they do not happen in the context of Mark's narrative. Jesus says to learn the lesson of the fig tree (which has just withered a little while before). He concludes by twice telling the disciples, and all (even us), to keep awake (Mark 13:35, 37).

". . . Calls Disciples . . ."

Much of Jesus' teaching is directed to his disciples. Even teaching that is addressed to the crowd or the Pharisees is explained to the disciples privately, often in a house. Jesus' relationship with his disciples is an important plot line in the narrative. After his baptism, receiving the Spirit, and triumphing over satanic temptation Jesus comes into Galilee proclaiming that the reign of God is drawing near, and he therefore summons people to "repent and believe in the gospel" (1:14-15). The first people to do so are the four fisherfolks Simon, Andrew, James, and John (1:16-20). Jesus first calls Simon and his brother Andrew, and they "immediately" leave their nets and follow Jesus. Jesus then "immediately" calls James and John the son of Zebedee, who express their repentance by "leaving their father in the boat with the hired servants," and who express their belief in the gospel by "going away after Jesus."

So begins the series of episodes I referred to previously as "from Capernaum to Capernaum," beginning with the exorcism in the synagogue and concluding with the healing of the paralytic in a house (1:21–2:12). Mark prefaces the next series of episodes with the call of Levi (2:15). After teaching the crowd by the sea, Jesus passes by Levi at his tax table and says, "Follow me." Levi gets up and follows Jesus. Levi then invites Jesus to dinner at his house along with other tax collectors "and sinners." The Pharisaic scribes complain, and they and Jesus and his disciples are off on a series of controversies over fasting, picking grain on the Sabbath, and healing on the Sabbath, which ends in the Pharisees conspiring for Jesus' destruction (2:18–3:6).

Jesus then goes with his disciples to the sea, where he attends to the needs of a crowd (3:7). He then goes up a mountain (3:13, recalling significant mountains in the Hebrew Scriptures, such as Mount Sinai, where the Hebrews received the Law: see Exod 19:3-25). Twice in this episode on the mountain Mark says that Jesus appointed twelve (echoing the twelve tribes of Israel). First he says that Jesus named them apostles. As apostles they are to be with Jesus, to be sent out (the literal meaning of "apostle") to preach his message (that the reign of God draws near, Mark 1:15), and to have authority to cast out demons (like Jesus, 1:27). (Jesus does in fact send them out later, two by two, and they "cast out many demons," 6:7-13.) The second time Mark says that Jesus appointed twelve, he lists the names (3:13-19). He begins with the three Jesus often takes into private spaces (such as Jairus' house, 5:37, the mount of transfiguration, 9:2, and Gethsemane, 14:33). These three are marked off because Jesus gave them new names: Peter ("Rock") for Simon, and Boanerges, or "Sons of Thunder," for James and John, the sons of Zebedee. Mark does not explain why Jesus gave them these names. He just goes on to the rest of the Twelve, which surprisingly does not include Levi, whose call was narrated just a few episodes before. The last person mentioned is Judas Iscariot, "who handed him over" (3:19). In this narrative aside Mark gives us the first indication that the Twelve will not "believe in the gospel" as fervently as we might hope.

An important element of the disciples' being with Jesus is to be insiders to Jesus' teaching. Jesus explains the parables to them privately, often in a house (4:11, 34; 7:17; 9:28; 10:10-11). Yet soon it becomes apparent that the disciples are not really "with Jesus," especially in the three boat crossings. In the first (4:35-41), which immediately precedes the Gerasene exorcism, Jesus sleeps during the storm, and the disciples accuse him of being unconcerned. After calming the storm, Jesus asks them, "Why are you so cowardly? Don't you have faith yet?" The implied answer is, no, they don't have faith, because they "fear a great fear," and they say to each other, "Who then is this that even the wind and sea are subject to him?" They don't know, but we do. We have read what Mark and God have said: Jesus is Son of God. We have information the characters do not have. We know more than the disciples do, for they have not read Mark's statement that Jesus is Son of God, nor have they heard God's voice at the baptism that Jesus is God's beloved Son. We've read those things, though, so we know who Jesus is.

In the second sea crossing (6:45-52) Jesus walks on water, and when the disciples see Jesus they are terrified and astounded because they did not understand about the loaves Jesus has just multiplied to feed the multitude and, like the Pharisees who want to destroy Jesus (3:5-6), their hearts are hardened. How the mighty have fallen!

In the third sea crossing (8:14-20) Jesus does not perform a miracle, but he does discuss the feeding miracles. Though the disciples have witnessed two multiplications of loaves, they are worried that they do not have any bread. (They do have one loaf, in fact.) Jesus asks them a series of rhetorical questions, which repeat Mark's charge in the second crossing that their hearts are hardened and indicate that they are now among the outsiders because they do not see or understand (see 4:11-12). Jesus then asks questions about the two feedings, which they answer correctly, and then he says, "Do you not yet understand?!" The disciples are silent here; Mark robs them of a voice because in fact they do not understand.

The next section in the narrative, as I have noted, is bracketed by healings of blind men. At Bethsaida, Jesus needs two tries to heal (8:22-26). First Jesus spits into the man's eyes, puts his hands on him, and asks if he can see. He says, "I see people, but I see them like trees walking." Jesus puts his hands on him again and looks intently at him, and he "sees all things clearly." The other healing (10:45-52) takes place as Jesus and his disciples are passing through Jericho on their way to Jerusalem. Blind Bartimaeus calls for Jesus, "son of David," to be compassionate toward him. Jesus calls him, he throws off his cloak, and Jesus asks him what he wants. Bartimaeus says that he wants to see again. Jesus tells him, "Go, your faith has saved you," which is what he also told the woman with a hemorrhage (5:34). "Immediately" he gets his sight back and follows Jesus "on the way" to Jerusalem, where Jesus will die.

Between these two healings are three sections in which Jesus first predicts his suffering, then the disciples misunderstand, and finally Jesus teaches them. In the first section (8:27–9:1), after Peter says that Jesus is the Christ and Jesus "rebukes" him by hushing him up, Jesus tells his disciples that "the son of humanity" is going to suffer, be rejected, be killed, and after three days rise. Peter rebukes Jesus for this, and then Jesus rebukes Peter, calling him Satan. He then teaches all the disciples about the necessity of taking up the cross and following him.

The second section of prediction, misunderstanding, and teaching (9:30-37) follows the transfiguration, in which God says to listen to his beloved son, and the exorcism of a boy with an unclean spirit, whom the disciples could not heal. Jesus again predicts his suffering, in slightly briefer terms than before. This time, however, the disciples are arguing "on the way" about who is the greatest. In a house in Capernaum Jesus teaches them that the first must be last and the servant. Immediately following this teaching, John attempts to stop an exorcist who was using Jesus' name though he was not a disciple, which leads to more teaching about not causing others to stumble (9:38-50). Soon after, the disciples rebuke parents bringing children to Jesus, but he says not to stop them, for the reign of God belongs to such (10:13 16). Then a man comes up to Jesus to ask him what to do for eternal life. Jesus tells him to observe the commandments, and when he says that he has, Jesus tells him to sell all he has and follow Jesus. The man does not do it, however, apparently because he is rich. The disciples do not understand Jesus' saying that it's difficult for the rich to enter into the reign of God. Peter says that they have left everything to follow Jesus, and Jesus assures them that they will be repaid in the present and the future.

With the third section (10:32-45), we wonder how well the disciples are following Jesus. He gives the most detailed prediction yet, saying that the religious leaders would condemn him to death and hand him over to the Gentiles, that is, the Romans, who would torture him and kill him, but he would rise after three days. James and John then "thunder" their requests for seats on either side of Jesus "in glory." Jesus then teaches about the greatest being the servant, as modeled by the son of humanity, who came to serve and to give his life as a ransom for many.

The disciples do not seem to get it. But the worst is yet to come! At the supper, in which Jesus says that his blood is poured out "for many," he predicts one disciple's betrayal, all the disciples' desertion (quoting from the Hebrew prophet Zechariah), and Peter's denial (14:12-31). While Jesus prays three times in Gethsemane about his coming suffering, Peter, James, and John fall asleep (14:32-42). And when Jesus is arrested, the Scripture is indeed fulfilled: Jesus' followers forsake him and flee (14:49-50). We see total and utter discipleship failure!

But maybe there is hope! On his way to Gethsemane, Jesus says that after his resurrection he will go ahead of the disciples into Galilee. And to the women who have come to anoint Jesus' body, the young man at the empty tomb repeats that promise, adding that the disciples will see Jesus there (16:7). Yet one wonders about this because the women flee from the tomb, just as the disciples fled from Jesus at his arrest, and they do not say anything to anyone, for they are afraid (16:8). This is where Mark's narrative ends. (The various endings that are probably in brackets in your Bible,

16:9-20, were added later.) Who would go tell that Jesus had been raised? Who would go see Jesus in Galilee? I guess it is up to us, the readers.

". . . Yet in Doing So He Meets Opposition, Which Leads to His Being Rejected . . ."

A story nearly always contains conflict, which propels the plot. Mark's story is filled with conflict, and we have noted much of that as we have discussed Mark's plot. In his miracles Jesus does battle with both human and superhuman forces. The exorcisms represent Jesus' entering into conflict with satanic forces and emerging victorious. In these exorcisms, though, as well as in the healings on the Sabbath, Jesus also enters into conflict with the scribes and the Pharisees who, like the demons, resist the reign of God. Another irony in Mark's story is that the religious authorities, whom one would expect to embrace Jesus' teaching, are his most vicious opponents. Indeed, the scribes and Pharisees conspire to do away with Jesus! Following his healing on the Sabbath, the Pharisees plot to kill Jesus (3:6), but they actually do not carry out their plan. The scribes, however, join with the chief priests in Jerusalem in handing over Jesus to the Roman governor Pontius Pilate, who has him crucified, just as Jesus predicted (10:33-34; see 14:1, 43, 53-65; 15:1). They flog Jesus, mock him, spit on him, and finally kill him (15:15-20).

But the religious authorities are not the only ones who let us down. Indeed, those we would expect to be on Jesus' side turn out to be his opponents. First the Nazarenes, folks in Jesus' home town, become his opponents. They are "scandalized" at Jesus. They ask several questions, such as "Where are these teachings from?" and "Isn't this the carpenter, the son of Mary and brother of James and Joses and Judas and Simon?" (6:2-3). (We know, of course, because we have read the story up to now. This is the Son of God, who gets his teachings from the Spirit of God. The Nazarenes, however, do not know that.) Because of their unbelief, which amazes him, Jesus is not able to do any works of power, although he does heal a few people (6:5-6). Second, Jesus' family opposes him, for they come to get him because people are saying he is crazy (3:21). Jesus' mother and brothers and sisters do not join Jesus' "true family," that is, his followers, who do God's will (3:31-35). Third, Jesus' own disciples become his opponents, as they misunderstand and become hard-hearted. And they desert him at his arrest (14:50). (Again, how ironic! Jesus appointed them to be with him, but at the moment of his greatest need they are not with him!)

". . . and Killed . . ."

The death of Jesus (15:21-41) is the central episode in the narrative. We should not be surprised when it happens, for Mark has been warning us throughout the story. He gives us a hint at Jesus' baptism, when God calls Jesus his beloved son, echoing language God uses when commanding Abraham to sacrifice Isaac (1:11; see Gen. 22:2). At the end of the controversy stories toward the beginning of the narrative, the Pharisees plot with the Herodians to kill Jesus (Mark 3:6). And soon after, Mark ends the list of disciples with Judas Iscariot, "who handed him over" (3:19). Then, of course, in the middle section of the narrative Jesus predicts his death three times. The disciples do not understand, but we understand. We have followed Jesus all the way to the cross.

We are not the only ones, however, even though the disciples have fled. Simon of Cyrene, who is simply passing by, is forced to carry Jesus' cross. In so doing he denies himself and follows Jesus (15:21; see 8:34). The women who followed Jesus in Galilee and served him (like the angels and like Simon's mother-in-law, 1:13, 31) watch the crucifixion (and burial) from afar (15:41, 47). Unlike other women in the gospel, they are named: Mary Magdalene, Mary the mother of James the younger and of Joses, and Salome. Mark also notes that "many other women went up with Jesus into Jerusalem" (15:41). In many ways the women replace the disciples here.

Throughout the narrative Mark has been quoting from or alluding to the Hebrew Scriptures. (When he quotes from them he is quoting from the Greek translation, known as the Septuagint, which many New Testament writers use.) Mark establishes himself as writing from within the tradition of the Hebrew Scriptures. It is the text behind the text, the text that gives meaning to his text. Mark's association with the Hebrew Scriptures begins in the opening lines of the gospel, as he quotes from Isaiah (and others: 1:2-3). A little later, God's words to the newly baptized Jesus echo Psalms, Isaiah, and Genesis. In the same way, the Hebrew Scriptures here give meaning to Jesus' death. Mark notes that darkness came "over the whole earth" (15:33), which echoes a number of prophetic texts Jesus refers to in his final speech. The coming of the son of humanity would be prefaced by the darkening of the sun and moon, which is now happening at the death of Jesus. The Psalms (especially Psalm 22) seem to be particularly prominent in the story of Jesus' crucifixion. Jesus here becomes the righteous sufferer often depicted in the Psalms: he is offered vinegar (Mark 15:23, Ps 69:21); his clothes are divided by casting lots (Mark 15:24; Ps 22:18); people mock him and shake their heads (Mark 15:29, 31; Ps 22:7). Jesus himself quotes the opening line of one of the Psalms (Mark 15:34; Ps 22:1): "My God, my God, why have you forsaken me?" It is so important for Mark that he quotes it in Jesus' language, Aramaic, and then translates it. (This is the fifth time Mark has quoted Jesus using Aramaic: first in resuscitating Jairus' daughter, 5:41; second in condemning a Pharisaic practice, 7:11; third in healing the deaf man, 7:34; and fourth in praying to God in Gethsemane, 14:36.) Mark does not expect us to know Aramaic, but he does expect us to know the Hebrew Scriptures well enough that we realize that this psalm begins with the expression of suffering (Ps 22:1-21a), but ends with the celebration of deliverance (Ps 22:21b-31). Jesus is the righteous sufferer who, even in the midst of death, expects God's deliverance.

Jesus dies, and Mark tells of two responses. First, the Temple curtain is ripped, presumably by God (Mark 15:38). This echoes the scene at the baptism, when the heavens were ripped (1:10). Is this the beginning of the destruction of the Temple, which Jesus foretold? (13:2). The second response is that the centurion says that Jesus was God's son (15:39). This also echoes the baptism, for there God called Jesus beloved son (1:11). The centurion is the only human character in the narrative to make this statement; the disciples never do. (Another irony! The one who supervises Jesus' execution is the only human to realize his identity as Son of God. But it doesn't lead to discipleship, for he later confirms for Pilate that Jesus is in fact dead.) With the centurion's statement at Jesus' death that Jesus was God's son, the "messianic secret" is broken: Jesus is the Messiah, who cannot come down from the cross (15:32; also 8:29-33); he is the son of humanity, who has been rejected and killed (8:31; 9:30; 10:33-34); and primarily he is the Son of God who has been crucified. At the beginning and end of the story, that is, at the baptism and at the crucifixion, there is a ripping and a voice calling Jesus God's son. So we have an inclusion surrounding the entire narrative. For us the readers (and hearers) Mark wraps (and rips!) his whole story in a package proclaiming that Jesus is the crucified Son of God.

". . . but God Raises Him."

But the story is not over. Jesus has predicted not only that he will die but that he will be raised. This is the deliverance he has been expecting. He even tells the disciples that they will see him in Galilee (14:28). But they do not, at least in the narrative. Indeed, nobody sees the risen Jesus anywhere! The women prove to be no more faithful in obeying Jesus than the disciples. All during the narrative Jesus has been telling people not to tell, and they go tell anyway. For example, Jesus tells a healed leper not to tell anyone, yet he "preaches the word" so much that Jesus can't go into a city any more (1:44-45). When Jesus heals a deaf man he tells the onlookers not to tell anybody, but they preach it all the more (7:36). Now a young man tells people to tell, and they do not tell. They are not faithful, but fearful.

Why would Mark end his story in such a way? Perhaps he wants us to meet Jesus in our Galilees. Or perhaps he does not want to compromise in any way the starkness and centrality of the crucifixion. It is here and only here that Jesus is Son of God.

Conclusion

We have looked at Mark's story through my plot statement, which I will repeat:

> Jesus the Son of God works miracles, teaches, and calls disciples, yet in doing so he meets opposition, which leads to his being rejected and killed, but God raises him.

Mark's story is plot-driven. But we have not just traced the plot in a linear fashion; we have also looked at layers. We have looked at patterns and repetitions and allusions. Mark is deep! We have looked at some of his story's depth. For example, he arranges the material in his story so carefully. Also, his story is so full of references to the Hebrew Scriptures.

Now that we have looked at Mark's whole story, we will look at the Gerasene's place in it.

CHAPTER THREE

Recovering from "Legionnaire's Disease":
The Story of the Gerasene's Exorcism

I'm going to tell you a story again.

This time it's a little story within the big story, that is, the little story of the Gerasene demoniac within the big story of Mark's gospel. Actually, the Gerasene's story is not that little; it's the longest single miracle story in the entire gospel. And Mark's story is not that big. It's the shortest of the four gospels. Anyway, in the last chapter we looked at Mark's whole story, the story of the crucified son of God, a story that begins with power but ends with suffering. In this chapter we are looking at the "little picture," the story of the exorcism of the Gerasene demoniac. We will first look at the context of this story in Mark's story. Then we will look at the structure of the story, especially as a "type scene." Finally, we will tell the story from a narrative-critical perspective.

The Story in Context

We discussed Mark's whole story in the previous chapter, but as we approach our focus—the story of the Gerasene demoniac—it is important that we reconnect with our context.

Mark's story, then, is often divided into two major sections. In the first section (1:14–8:21) the focus is on Jesus' miracles, on his POWER. In the second major section (8:22–15:47) the focus is on Jesus' death, on his SUFFERING. The story of the Gerasene appears in the "power" section of the gospel. Exactly how does Jesus demonstrate his power in this section? After calling his disciples, Jesus goes working miracles from "Capernaum to Capernaum," beginning with the exorcism in the synagogue, continuing with the healings of Simon's mother-in-law and a leper, and ending with the healing of a paralytic lowered through the roof (1:21–2:12). Jesus and his disciples then find themselves in controversy, involving eating with sinners, fasting, and Sabbath activities, ending with the Sabbath healing of a man with a withered hand (2:13–3:6).

Jesus then separates insiders from outsiders. He appoints twelve insiders who will be with him and will go out to exorcize (3:13-19). Jesus says the scribes are outsiders, for they say he exorcizes through an unclean spirit rather than the Holy Spirit. Jesus' family members also become outsiders, for they are coming to get him because people are saying he's crazy. Jesus says that his true family, the real insiders, include the ones sitting around him, doing God's will (3:34-35). Jesus continues separating insiders and outsiders through his teaching in parables (4:1-34). He says he tells parables to the crowd, but he explains them to the disciples, for the mystery of God's reign has been given to them (4:11; also 4:33-34). The disciples are the insiders, while the crowd consists of outsiders.

With his insiders Jesus crosses the Sea of Galilee. He demonstrates his power on both sides of the sea, both the Jewish and the Gentile sides. Mark tells us about three sea crossing scenes, the first two of which involve miracles. They demonstrate the power of Jesus but also the seeming powerlessness of the disciples. In the first sea crossing, in which Jesus calms the sea, the disciples are fearful and faithless (4:35-41). In the next crossing, in which Jesus walks on water, they are terrified and astounded; they fail to understand about the feeding miracle, and their hearts are hardened (6:45-52). After the feeding of the four thousand, Jesus and his disciples are again in a boat crossing the sea, and at Jesus' mention of "the leaven of the Pharisees and Herod" they worry about the lack of bread in the boat. Jesus asks them a number of rhetorical questions, implying that they do not perceive or understand and that their hearts are hardened. Jesus then says, "Do you still not understand?" The implied answer is, no, they do not. Even though they have been given the mystery of God's reign, they do not get it (8:14-21).

Also in this section are Jesus' two feeding miracles, one to five thousand on the Jewish side and the other to four thousand on the Gentile side (6:30-44; 8:1-10). Jesus also teaches about purity (7:1-23) and demonstrates it by healing the demon-possessed daughter of the Syrophoenician woman (7:24-29). The disciples are not completely powerless, for Jesus sends them out to preach, heal, and cast out demons, which they do (6:7-13).

This subsection of the gospel, which is bracketed by the three sea crossings, begins with a sequence of four stories in which Jesus demonstrates his power. Jesus first calms the sea (4:35-41), then he casts out a legion of demons in Gerasa (5:1-20). He then heals a woman with a hemorrhage and raises Jairus' daughter (5:21-43). As we noted in the previous chapter, the story of the woman with a hemorrhage is sandwiched, or "intercalated," within the story of Jairus' daughter.

Let us look at these two miracle stories that precede and follow the Gerasene exorcism. First we come to the calming of the sea (4:35-41). After completing his parable speech to the crowd, Jesus, who is already in the boat, tells his disciples to go to the other side of the sea. While en route, their boat is buffeted by a great windstorm. The disciples awaken the sleeping Jesus with the words, "Teacher, don't you care that we're perishing?" Jesus gets up and rebukes the wind and says to the sea, "Silent, be quiet," not unlike what he did and said to the demoniac in the synagogue in Capernaum (1:25). The wind stops, and there is a great calm. (First there is a "great" windstorm and then a "great" calm.) Jesus says to his disciples, "Why are you cowardly? Don't you have any faith yet?" They are then afraid, or literally, "they feared a great fear," and they ask one another, "Who then is this that even the wind and the sea obey him?" Hmm, the disciples do not seem to get it. They have left their families and their livelihood to follow Jesus; he has appointed them to be with him, to preach and cast out demons; he has given them the mystery of God's reign and has explained the parables for them. Yet during a storm on the lake they are fearful and faithless. They do not even know who Jesus is. However, we know because the narrator, God, and the demons have told us. Jesus is God's Spirit-endowed Son.

Following the exorcism of the Gerasene, Jesus and his disciples return to the Galilean side of the sea where they are met by a "great" crowd, which includes a synagogue leader named Jairus who begs Jesus to lay hands on his deathly ill daughter. While Jesus is on the way there, a woman emerges out of the "great crowd." She has been hemorrhaging for twelve years. She touches Jesus' clothes and is healed. Somewhat comically, Jesus, aware of a release of power, asks who touched him. The woman tells him, and Jesus says that her faith has saved her. Jairus is then informed that his daughter is dead, but Jesus tells him to believe, not fear. Jesus leads Peter, James, and John into Jairus' house, where he takes the girl by the hand and says to her in Aramaic, "Little girl, get up." She gets up and begins to walk around. Mark notes that she is twelve years old. People are amazed, but Jesus tells them not to say anything to anyone.

A number of themes appear in this series of four miracle stories. Perhaps the primary one is Jesus' power over the elements, over the demons (even a legion of them), over longstanding illness, and even over death itself. What power this Spirit-endowed Son of God has! Another important theme is faith over against fear. Jesus' word to Jairus, "Don't be afraid; just believe" (5:36), could be addressed to all the characters who are afraid in this series of stories: the disciples (4:40-41), the Gerasenes who see the man from whom Jesus has expelled a legion of demons (5:15), the woman healed of her hemorrhage (5:33), and Jairus (5:36). These last two serve as examples of characters who move from fear to faith. Jesus says it explicitly to the woman: "Daughter, your faith has saved you. Go in peace and be healed of your disease" (5:34).

The Story's Structure

Having considered the context, we now turn our attention to the structure. The story of the exorcism of the Gerasene demoniac is a "type scene"; that is, it has a particular format that appears repeatedly in the gospel. It helps the readers and hearers remember.[1] The type scene of this particular story is exorcism. There are three such exorcisms in the gospel. In addition to this story of the Gerasene, there is the exorcism of the man with an unclean spirit in the synagogue at Capernaum near the beginning of the gospel (Jesus' first miracle, 1:21-28), and the deaf and mute boy near the middle of the gospel, immediately following the transfiguration (9:14-29). (I said in the previous chapter that there were four exorcisms, and I included the exorcism of the Syrophoenician's daughter, 7:24-30. That one really fits better into the type scene of a healing because it is quite different in form from the other three.)

It is interesting to compare these other two exorcisms with that of the Gerasene. Let's first note similarities. In all three stories persons are said to have an unclean spirit (1:23; 5:2; 9:25). Furthermore, in all three the demoniac screams, usually when the demon is exiting (1:26; 9:26), though the Gerasene screams continually, even when addressing Jesus for the first time (5:5, 7). In all three the initiative for the encounter is with the demoniac, or, in the case of the son, with the father (9:17; see 1:23; 5:6). Also in all three Mark tells us about the reaction to the exorcism. With the first two exorcisms people are amazed (1:27; 5:20), though the initial response by the Gerasenes to the exorcism is fear (5:15). Mark does not tell us the general reaction to the exorcism of the son, for his interest is in the disciples' response, which they express "in the house" to Jesus. He says they weren't able to cast out the demon because they didn't pray (9:29).

---

[1] For more on type scenes in Mark see David Rhoads, Joanna Dewey, and Donald Michie, *Mark as Story: An Introduction to the Narrative of a Gospel* (2nd ed. Minneapolis: Fortress, 1999) 51. For type scenes in the Hebrew Scriptures see the very helpful discussion in Robert Alter, *The Art of Biblical Narrative* (New York: Basic Books, 1981) 47–62.

Beyond these general similarities, the Gerasene's exorcism is quite similar to the one that takes place in Capernaum. They are both placed in key positions in the gospel. The Capernaum exorcism is the first miracle in Jewish territory and the Gerasene exorcism is the first in Gentile territory. Furthermore, both characters appear on the scene "suddenly" (1:23; 5:2), and both scream at Jesus (1:23; 5:6). Additionally, they say much the same thing. The demoniac in Capernaum says:

> What've you got against us, Jesus of Nazareth?
> Have you come to destroy us?
> I know who you are, the holy one of God. (1:24)

The Gerasene says,

> What've you got against me, Jesus son of the highest God?
> I swear to you by God, don't torture me! (5:7)

Each begins, "What've you got against me/us?" (It is interesting to note that the Capernaum man speaks of "us" while the Gerasene speaks of "me," though in Capernaum there is only one unclean spirit and the Gerasene has a legion of them.) Then each calls Jesus by name with some descriptor. Each speaks of some aggressive act toward the demonic. Finally, each notes Jesus' relationship with God.

With that the similarities end. The setting is quite different. The Capernaum exorcism happens in a synagogue in Galilee, while the Gerasene exorcism takes place on the "other side of the sea" from Galilee. Mark does not tell us about the Capernaum man's behavior prior to coming to Jesus, while he tells us much about the Gerasene. At Capernaum Jesus rebukes the unclean spirit (just as he rebukes the unclean spirit of the son, 9:25) and tells him to be quiet and to come out of the man (1:25). Though Jesus is about to say similar words to the Gerasene, "Come out of the man, you unclean spirit" (5:8), apparently he does not speak them because he wants to engage the man in dialogue about his name. When he does actually cast the demons out, Mark simply says that he accedes to the demons' request to go into the pigs (5:13). At Capernaum the spirit convulses the man and makes him cry out (which is what happens to the son with the unclean spirit, 9:26), while no such histrionics are described for the Gerasene. We hear no more about this man at Capernaum after the spirit leaves him, while we hear much about the Gerasene, who is "seated, dressed, and sane" (5:15) and wants to be with Jesus but is instead sent out to preach (5:18-20). (Indeed, the exorcism becomes a commissioning story!)

Let us now compare the exorcism of the Gerasene with that of the son with a spirit, beginning with the similarities. We do have a description of the son's malady, not unlike what we have with the Gerasene. His father testifies that the spirit makes the son unable to speak, throws him down, makes him foam at the mouth and grind his teeth, and "withers" him (which is what happens to the fig tree, 11:21; the NRSV translates this word in regard to the son as "becomes rigid," 9:18). Indeed, the spirit confirms what the father has just said by "suddenly" (that word again, which appears in all three exorcism stories) convulsing him and making him roll on the ground and foam at the mouth (9:20). The father tells Jesus that the spirit has afflicted his son "from childhood" (9:21) and that it often throws him into fire and water with the intent to kill him (9:22). The Gerasene also engages in self-mutilating behavior, gashing himself with stones (5:5). Indeed, in both circumstances the demon operates independently of the person who has it. The unclean spirit seizes and convulses the son, which it does when it "sees" Jesus (9:18, 20). The Gerasene demons negotiate with Jesus their departure from the man and entrance into the pigs (5:12).

Now we turn to the differences: The father of the demoniac initiates the encounter with Jesus, while the Gerasene demoniac initiates the encounter. The son does not speak at all, because the unclean spirit renders him unable to speak. So the father does all the talking. The Gerasene, of course, speaks for himself. The son demonstrates his deviant behavior in front of Jesus, while the Gerasene does not give Jesus the (dis)pleasure. After the unclean spirit leaves the son he appears dead, and Jesus takes his hand and lifts him up (9:26-27), while Mark does not tell us about what happened "immediately" to the Gerasene when the demons left him. Eventually, though, he does appear "seated, dressed, and sane" (5:15). Indeed, this exorcism echoes two previous healings, the raising of Jairus' daughter and the exorcism at a distance of the Syrophoenician's daughter, where a parent intercedes for a child. Furthermore, Jairus' daughter, like the son in this story, appeared dead, and Jesus took her hand (5:39, 42).

Perhaps the biggest difference is that the exorcism of the son becomes another lesson in the misunderstanding of the disciples, while the exorcism of the Gerasene proceeds with no mention at all of the disciples. In the former story Jesus, along with Peter, James, and John, returns to the rest of his disciples following the transfiguration. The scribes are arguing with the disciples, with a "great crowd" looking on. When Jesus asks what they are arguing about, the father says that he brought his son to Jesus' disciples to cast out the unclean spirit, but they couldn't do it. Jesus complains about this "unfaithful generation," apparently referring to the disciples, who have already demonstrated that they lack faith. Jesus then takes up the son's case. Afterward Jesus enters a house, and the disciples have another private question-and-answer session with their teacher. They ask why they couldn't cast out the unclean spirit, and Jesus says that such a spirit won't come out except through prayer. And we later learn in Gethsemane (14:38-40) that the disciples don't do so well with prayer!

We have here a type scene, an exorcism, which is the same as but different from the two other exorcisms in the gospel. Like other exorcisms, it can be divided into four subsections: setting, encounter, exorcism, reaction.

Setting	Jesus and his disciples go across the sea.
Encounter	A man with an unclean spirit meets him. Prior to this he could not be restrained, but roamed the region, howling and cutting himself. Jesus asks the man his name, and the man tells him.
Exorcism	The man begs Jesus not to send them out of the region. The spirits ask to be sent into the pigs, and Jesus does so. The pigs drown in the sea.
Reaction	Pig-grazers go tell what has happened, and people come to see Jesus and the man, leading them to be afraid and ask Jesus to leave the region. The man asks Jesus to be with him, but Jesus tells him to go home and tell what has happened, so the man goes to the Ten Cities to preach, and people are amazed.

We see much movement in this story. A man with an unclean spirit rushes at Jesus and falls down before him. The demon-possessed pigs rush off a bank into the sea. The pig-grazers run off to tell what has happened. The people come out to see. And when Jesus tells the man to go home and tell, he goes and preaches in all the neighboring cities. With all this stormy movement, Jesus is the still center. People come to him and then run away.

As Ann-Janine Morey has noted, the prepositions "out" and "in" are prominent in this story.[2] "Out" dominates in the first half of the story, but "in" in the second. Jesus goes "out" of the boat, and the man meets him "out" of the tombs. Jesus was about to tell the unclean spirit to come "out" of the man. He begs Jesus not to send them "out" of the region, but rather to send them "into" the pigs, so that the spirits go "out" and "into" the pigs, which go "into" the sea and are drowned "in" the sea. The pig-grazers go

---

[2] Ann-Janine Morey, "The Old In/Out," in Robert Detweiler and William G. Doty, eds., *The Daemonic Imagination: Biblical Text and Secular Story,* AAR Studies in Religion 60 (Atlanta: Scholars, 1990) 172–73.

tell what happened "in" the city and the country. The people beg Jesus to get "out" of their country, so he gets "into" the boat. The healed man goes preaching "in" the Ten Cities. A lot of energy is going out and in.

Also note the emotional reaction of folks. The Gerasenes are afraid when they see that the man who had had a legion of demons is now dressed and sane. Additionally, people in the Decapolis are amazed when they hear the man proclaim what Jesus has done for him. It seems that Mark wants us to have an emotional (yet faithful!) response to the story, too.

The Story

We now pursue a close narrative-critical reading of the story, using the structure above to frame the discussion. We will follow the structure I set out earlier: setting, encounter, exorcism, reaction.

1. Setting

First, Jesus and his disciples come to the "other side of the sea" (5:1). In the previous episode Jesus has expressed his intention to go to the other side (4:35), and now they have made it. The sea provides an important setting for the gospel narrative. Jesus calls disciples as he is passing along by the sea (1:16-20; 2:13). He heals and teaches by the sea (3:7; 4:1). Jesus and his disciples have just made their first trip across the sea, in which Jesus has calmed a storm (4:35-41).

Mark further explains that the other side of the sea is "the region of the Gerasenes." We often see such "two-step progressions" in the gospel.[3] Mark will first say something, and then explain it. He does that at the beginning of his gospel, in which he calls "Jesus Christ" "son of God" (1:1). We will see such two-step progressions twice more in this story. When Jesus asks the man his name, he says "Legion," and then explains, "for we're many" (5:9). (Many of Mark's two-step progressions begin with "for" in the second stage.) Additionally, the man begs Jesus not to send the demons out of the region. Then the demons themselves beg to go into a herd of pigs (5:10, 12).

This "other side of the sea" does represent an "otherness" for Mark. There is a "this side of the sea," that is, Galilee, and there is the "other side of the sea," that is, the Gerasenes. This "other side" is strange and foreign for Mark. His world is dualistic: clean/unclean, Jew/Gentile, heaven/earth, insiders/outsiders, and this side/the other side. One of these two is better than the others. So Jesus leaves the familiar territory of "this side of the

---

[3] For more on "two-step progressions" see Rhoads, Dewey, and Michie, *Mark as Story,* 49–51.

sea" to go to "the other side." The suspense begins to build. Jesus has had success on "this side" of the sea, but what about on "the other side"?

On the other side, Jesus gets out of the boat (5:2). The boat is an important part of the setting, because this is how Jesus navigates the sea. Jesus twice had to use it because of the crowd (3:9; 4:1). He uses the boat as his setting for teaching parables (4:2). The boat carries Jesus where he needs to go in order to proclaim that the reign of God is drawing near. It takes him across the sea (4:36). He feels comfortable enough in it that he falls asleep in the midst of a storm (4:37-38). In our story, Jesus' getting out of and into the boat (5:2, 18) forms an inclusion that brackets the episode.

2. Encounter

"Suddenly," as soon as Jesus gets out of the boat, a man with an unclean spirit meets him (5:2). We have certainly seen the word "suddenly" before, especially with miracle stories. The man with an unclean spirit appears suddenly in the synagogue in Capernaum (1:23); the leprosy leaves the leper suddenly after Jesus' command (1:42); the paralytic suddenly takes up his mat (2:12); after Jesus heals the man with a withered hand, the Pharisees suddenly conspire to kill Jesus (3:6). Mark carries us away with the speed and force of his narrative, especially the miracle stories.

This man comes suddenly "out of the tombs." Tombs are mentioned three times in this story. The first two appear in successive lines, framing the first mention of the man with an unclean spirit (5:2, 3). This is another example of Mark's two-stage progression, for he first states that the man came out of the tombs and then he explains that he was living among the tombs. This is certainly "the other side," for the tombs are unclean places for Jews. (Mark expects us to be familiar with Jewish customs and the Hebrew Scriptures to know this; see Lev 21:1; 22:4-5; Isa 65:4).[4]

So the unclean spirit has brought the man into unclean places. Jesus has met people with unclean spirits before, such as the one in the synagogue at Capernaum at the beginning of his Galilean ministry (Mark 1:21-28) and those in summaries (1:32-33, 39; 3:11). An "unclean" spirit, as opposed to a clean, or "holy" spirit, is another indication of Mark's dualistic worldview.

To show the desperate conditions of this man, Mark takes us back in time a bit, not unlike what he does a little later with the woman with a hemorrhage (5:26), though Mark lingers a long while with the Gerasene. Indeed, just as Mark told about the windstorm on the sea in some detail in the

---

[4] Mary Ann Tolbert, "Introduction and Annotations to the Gospel According to Mark," in Walter J. Harrelson, ed., *The New Interpreter's Study Bible: New Revised Standard Version with the Apocrypha* (Nashville: Abingdon, 2003) 1816.

episode preceding this one (4:37), so in the same way he gives a detailed description of the Gerasene here. Mark tells first about his attempted binding (5:3-4) and then about loosing (5:5). The fact that no one could restrain or tame him is stated twice (5:3, 4), and these two "non-restraint clauses" frame statements about his being bound and then loosing himself from his chains and fetters. Mark mentions "chains" three times and "fetters" twice to show the strength of this man. He was bound, but he broke the bonds. No one was strong enough to tame this wild animal of a man. Again the tension builds. Will Jesus be strong enough? Mark has already given us a hint. In the earlier controversy with the Jerusalem scribes over the source of Jesus' exorcizing power, Jesus said, "No one can enter into a strong man's house to plunder his things unless one first binds the strong man" (3:27). Jesus, by the power of the Holy Spirit, is able to bind this strong man, though no one else has been able to do so. It is emblematic of his defeat of Satan.

Conflict first enters the story here, not between the demoniac and Jesus, though that will come. Conflict here is between the Gerasenes and the demoniac. They try to restrain him by chaining and fettering him. Exactly who is doing this? Mark doesn't say. And why? Again, he doesn't say. His purpose is to emphasize the unrestrained strength of the man and the alienation he experienced from his fellow townspeople.

This man cannot be bound by his fellow Gerasenes, but rather he looses himself to wander day and night (that is, all the time!) in the tombs and on the mountains. (It seems that these tombs are dug into the mountains.)[5] The tombs are places of the dead, while the mountain is a place of contact with the living God, where Jesus appoints disciples and prays (3:13; 6:46). But this man doesn't meet God on the mountains, at least not yet. In these places the man screams (as demoniacs are wont to do; 1:24, 26; 3:11; 9:26) and gashes himself with stones. (Is he screaming because he is cutting himself or simply because the demons are tormenting him?) This self-mutilation is also an "unclean" activity (see Deut 14:1).[6] (The son with an unclean spirit also engaged in self-destructive behavior: Mark 9:22.) Who is trying to hurt whom with the stones? Is the man trying to kill himself? Or is he trying to kill the demons? Or are the demons trying to kill him? Or is it possible to make such a distinction with one who has an unclean spirit? The man is not only in conflict with his townspeople, but also with himself.

---

[5] See John R. Donahue and Daniel J. Harrington, *The Gospel of Mark,* SP 2 (Collegeville: Liturgical Press, 2002) 163.

[6] Tolbert, "Introduction and Annotations," 1816.

Mark draws a very stark picture of this man. He is a strong man, strongly bound to uncleanness, to Satan, to death. He has our sympathy, even our empathy, as Mark describes his torment in such detail. Poor guy—living in tombs, being bound by townspeople, cutting himself! The suspense builds. Can Jesus heal him? We hope so.

With our sympathies with the man, and certainly with Jesus, Mark tries to catch up to story time. The man sees Jesus from a distance and runs to him. He falls down in front of Jesus, just as the unclean spirits at the seaside did (3:11). The man with an unclean spirit recognizes a superior power, one who has Holy Spirit. He screams, this time with a "great voice" (like the Capernaum demoniac and the crucified Jesus, 1:26; 15:34, 37), perhaps echoing the "great wind" on the sea earlier (4:37). His screaming words are similar to the unclean spirits at Capernaum and by the sea, who identified Jesus as the holy one of God and the Son of God (1:24; 3:11). Indeed, Mark said earlier that the demons knew Jesus (1:34).

The man asks what Jesus has against him, and he pleads with Jesus not to torture him. Jesus has nothing against the man, but much against the unclean spirit the man has. Jesus is not going to torture him (for the man has endured enough torture at his own hands and the hands of the Gerasenes), but Jesus, Son of (the highest) God, is going to deliver him. The main conflict in the story now emerges, between Jesus and the demons.

Jesus is about to say the same words he addresses to the other demoniacs (1:25; 9:25), but instead he engages the man in dialogue. Jesus asks him his name (5:9). Jesus has already given new names to Simon (Peter) and to James and John (Boanerges), his inner circle (3:16-17). Furthermore, someone who is not a disciple is casting out demons in Jesus' name (9:38). So Jesus wants to find out this man's name, something he does not do with any other demoniac in the gospel. Exactly what is Jesus up to? Perhaps he feels that he needs to know the man's name in order to gain power over him in this land on the "other side of the sea." Whatever the reason, the man says, "Legion's my name, for we're many." No wonder the man is doing such horrible things to himself. He has many demons, a legion of them! Ugh! Our sympathy for him increases. Mark probably expects us to recognize "Legion" as a Roman military term for about six thousand soldiers, soldiers occupying the Mediterranean world at the time. This man has a (Roman!) legion of demons; is Jesus powerful enough?

"Legion's *my* name, for *we*'re many." The demoniac alternates singular and plural, not unlike the man in Capernaum who says, "What do you have against us . . . ? Have you come to destroy us?" (1:24). With Legion's pronominal switch ("my/we"), which Mark repeats in the next line ("he/them"), the demoniac himself fades into the background, and the demons themselves charge into the foreground.

3. Exorcism

Having revealed his identity, Legion begs Jesus "wildly" not to send the "many" out of the region (5:10). This is unclean territory, perfect for an unclean spirit. Again there is a note of suspense. Where will they go? On the mountainside (now is his chance to encounter God) are a "great herd" of pigs—another indication that this is unclean territory, for Mark assumes we know that pigs are unclean animals (Lev 11:7-8; Deut 14:8; Isa 65:4).[7] So the unclean spirits "beg" Jesus, for they realize that his Holy Spirit is greater than their unclean spirit, that he might send them into the pigs. They don't need Legion to negotiate for them; they can negotiate for themselves. They're unclean spirits, so they can go into unclean animals! Jesus then lets them. Mark doesn't even give Jesus' words at this point. Jesus is the one with superior power, and he simply accedes to the demons' request. So the unclean spirits leave the man and go into the pigs. Unclean spirits in unclean animals!

But a strange thing happens! The herd of pigs, which Mark numbers at two thousand, as he continues to give more detail to this story, rushes down a steep bank into the sea. And they are drowned in the sea! Presumably the unclean spirits are drowned too. I'm sure they didn't "bank" on that! This is the same sea Jesus has just calmed, and now it has drowned the demons. This land is now clean!

4. Reaction

The people tending the pigs run off (as the demoniac ran toward Jesus), and they tell what has just happened "in the city and country" (5:14). They tell everywhere! So people come to see. They come to Jesus, who has initiated all this, and they see the demoniac, whom Mark identifies as "the man who had had the legion" (5:15, another two-step progression). (Demon-possessed, he had a name, but now he has none.) When he had the legion he was wandering, naked, and crazy. But now the people see him as "seated, dressed, and sane." Clothes are important for Mark. They indicate a changed status. When Jesus is transfigured, his clothes become quite white (9:3). When Bartimaeus comes to Jesus, he throws off his cloak (10:50). The young man at the empty tomb is dressed in white (16:5).[8] The young man at Jesus' arrest travels the opposite direction from the Gerasene; he is clothed with a linen cloth, but when he is seized, he runs

---

[7] Ibid.

[8] I am indebted to Steven Johnson for pointing me to the connection between the Gerasene's being clothed and other characters' being clothed (or not!) in Mark.

off naked! (14:51). The Gerasene's being clothed here indicates that something significant has happened to him! He is indeed no longer possessed by a legion of demons; he is sane.

This brief statement of the Gerasene's newfound condition contrasts sharply with the elaborate description of his behavior before the exorcism. But what more need be said? Mark says that he did all these horrible things before, but now they're stopped. We are relieved.

The Gerasenes, however, are afraid, just as the disciples were in the boat earlier (4:40-41). They have no faith. Then they hear about the pigs. Now, that's the last straw! They beg Jesus to get out of their country. Earlier the demons had begged Jesus so that they might stay in the country. Now the people want Jesus to leave. Even here on the other side of the sea, Jesus' exorcisms are a source of controversy. Resolution of conflict within the man and between Jesus and the demons leads to conflict between Jesus and the people. Jesus' opponents are both demonic and human. Just as scribes rejected him in Galilee and chief priests will reject him in Jerusalem, the Gerasenes reject him here.

Just as Jesus agreed to the demons' begging, he agrees to the people's begging. He gets into the boat he got out of earlier. A lot has happened since then! But the Gerasene, whom Mark now calls "the ex-demonized one" to emphasize for us his changed status, begs Jesus to be with him. All the others who have begged Jesus have gotten their way. And this man begs to be with Jesus. In other words, he wants to be a disciple, like the Twelve, who were appointed "to be with" Jesus (3:14). However, Jesus does not let him. It is the only time in this story that Jesus refuses anybody who begs him. The final conflict in the story, then, is between Jesus and the healed man. The man wants to be a disciple, but Jesus doesn't want him to. Why? Jesus has already appointed the Twelve, and they are Galilean Jews; they represent the twelve tribes of Israel. Furthermore, no one becomes a disciple on one's own initiative; one must be called. Additionally, Jesus has plans for the man. He tells him, in his first quoted words since asking the demoniac his name, "Go home," just as he had earlier told the healed paralytic to go home (2:11). And he adds, "to your own people." His own people? You mean the Gerasenes, who attempted to bind him and who just now chased Jesus out of town? Those people? Is Jesus here trying to resolve the conflict between the Gerasene and the townspeople? Jesus tells him to tell them "what the Lord has done for you and how he's had compassion on you." At other times when Jesus heals people, such as a leper, a twelve-year-old girl, and a man who couldn't hear, he tells them *not* to tell (1:44; 5:36; 7:36). There is no "messianic secret" here on "the other side of the sea."

What the man is to tell his people is "what the Lord has done for you and how he's had compassion on you." Jesus here reveals a hidden actor: the Lord, that is, the Lord God (see 1:3; 11:9; 12:11, 29-30, 36, 37; 13:20),[9] the highest God, to use the Gerasene's language. It is not Jesus who has cast out the demons from the man, but the Lord, who has given Jesus, his beloved Son, the Holy Spirit to bind the strong man and to proclaim the nearness of God's reign. In casting out the demons, the Lord God has had compassion on the man. Blind Bartimaeus calls for Jesus to "have compassion on him," and he does, by giving him his sight (10:47-48, 52). The Gerasene swears to God for Jesus not to torture him (5:7), and through Jesus, God has compassion on him and casts out his demons, thus making him sane.

The man goes away and doesn't just tell; he "preaches" (as John and Jesus did, 1:7, 14, and as the disciples would do, 6:12). And he doesn't go home, unless "home" is understood in a very broad sense. He goes away to preach in the Ten Cities. The Ten Cities, or the Decapolis, was the region around and including Gerasa. Was he avoiding going home? He goes away preaching in the Decapolis "what Jesus has done for him." But Jesus told him to tell what the Lord has done for him. Does a new conflict arise? Is the man being obedient or disobedient? Jesus told him to go home and tell his people what the Lord has done for him, but he goes to the Ten Cities and proclaims what Jesus has done for him. Characters in the gospel do not do so well with commands to tell or not to tell. As noted in the previous chapter, after Jesus heals the leper and the deaf man, respectively, he commands people not to tell, but they go tell anyway (1:45; 7:36). At the empty tomb the young man instructs the women to go tell the disciples that Jesus is going ahead of them to Galilee, but they don't do that (16:7-8). Is the Gerasene any better?

Everyone in the Ten Cities, however, is "amazed" at his proclamation. Mark often says that people are amazed, astonished, or astounded at Jesus. People at Capernaum are astonished at the casting out of a demon and the healing of the paralytic (1:27; 2:12), as are the disciples at the walking on water, at the transfiguration, and at going up to Jerusalem (6:51; 9:15; 10:32), as are people at Jesus' answers about taxes (12:17), as is Pilate at Jesus' silence (15:5), and as are the women at the empty tomb (16:5). It is particularly interesting to note that when Jesus returns to the Ten Cities and heals a deaf man, he commands the people to tell no one, but they "preach" it anyway and they (either the preachers or the preached to) are "astounded" (7:37). Characters are always amazed at Jesus, but this is not in and of itself a response of faith.

[9] Tolbert, "Introduction and Annotations," 1817.

Mark takes his narrative eye off the Gerasene and returns to Jesus going back to Galilee. What happens to the Gerasene? Does he ever go back home and tell his people? Is he ever reconciled to them? We don't know. Mark doesn't say. His narrative spotlight turned toward the Gerasene briefly, but he turns it back toward Jesus so he can narrate some more miracles in this series. It is, after all, the "Gospel of Jesus Christ, Son of God" (1:1).

Conclusion

The Gerasene might be called a "stock character" or "type."[10] He is one of a number of people who come to Jesus for healing, such as the woman with a hemorrhage, blind Bartimaeus, the Syrophoenician woman, and the leper. Though Mark's gospel is relatively short, he fills it with interesting characters. Although they are not lavishly described, Mark does "load a lot into a little." Compare our modern novels, in which there is great description, yet the characters are not quite as enticing as in Mark and the other gospels.

Because of the reserve with which Mark describes his characters it is all the more notable that he portrays the Gerasene in comparative detail. The Gerasene, then, is not "any old" stock character but, especially prior to his exorcism, a highly developed "stock character." It seems that Mark "lavishes" detail on him because of the importance of the exorcisms in the gospel. They are the way Jesus is entering the strong man's house, tying up the strong man, and plundering his goods (3:27).

But beyond that, the Gerasene is a Gentile, a man with an unclean spirit in an unclean territory. Yet this land has been cleansed by Jesus. Perhaps by describing the demoniac so vividly Mark is calling us to go with Jesus to "the other side of the sea." Jesus himself has prepared the way. As David Rhoads says about the Syrophoenician woman, "The story challenges the audience not to set limits on the universality of the good news of the kingdom of God. The whole first part of Mark's story prepares the hearer to go with Jesus across this final boundary to Gentile territory."[11]

We have come now to the end of the narrative-critical treatment of the story of the Gerasene demoniac. We said in Chapter 1 that narrative criticism was an important new way in which to understand the gospels. We

---

[10] See Rhoads, Dewey, and Michie, *Mark as Story*, 100–101; David Rhoads, "Jesus and the Syrophoenician Woman in Mark: A Narrative-Critical Study," *Journal of the American Academy of Religion* 62 (1994) 359.

[11] Rhoads, "Jesus and the Syrophoenician Woman in Mark," 370.

demonstrated in Chapter 2 that the Gospel of Mark could be understood as the story of the crucified Son of God. Here in this chapter we have seen that the story of the exorcism of the Gerasene demoniac plays a key role in the unfolding of Mark's story, for here on the other side of the sea Jesus demonstrates the nearness of God's reign by binding the strong man and plundering his house, thus cleansing this man and this land.

We have read the story against two backdrops, first that of the three Synoptic Gospels and then that of the Gospel of Mark. Then we read the story in and of itself. It is a great little story, isn't it? It takes on even more significance when it is read in context with the bigger story it is a part of and in context with the "same but different" other stories.

Though one task is done, our other task remains undone. We have given a narrative-critical treatment of the story of the Gerasene. But that is only half of our work. A soulful, psychological treatment still awaits us. So on we go.

PART II

Probing the Gerasene's Soul:
Psychological Biblical Criticism

CHAPTER FOUR

Legion's Unconscious Uncovered: Freud and Jung

Let me tell you another story.

I began Part 1 with a story about how I became interested in narrative criticism of the gospels, so I now begin Part 2 with a story about how I became interested in psychological criticism.

It was late spring 1985. I had just finished my doctoral dissertation, and I was to graduate in a few weeks. I was teaching at William Jewell College, a small Baptist college in suburban Kansas City, Missouri. I was ready to begin a new phase in my research. My dissertation on the Gospel of John had dealt with literary, historical, and theological issues.[1] What would I now research and write? Historical criticism and narrative criticism stimulated my mind, but they left my soul unaddressed. I had always been a seeker, both in my academic and personal life. I was striving for a depth I had not found.

I pulled down from my bookshelf a couple of books by Walter Wink that seemed to speak to my condition: *The Bible in Human Transformation: Toward a New Paradigm for Biblical Study*[2] and *Transforming Bible Study: A Leader's Guide*.[3] In the former book Wink proclaimed, "Historical

---

[1] It was later published as Michael E. Willett, *Wisdom Christology in the Fourth Gospel* (San Francisco: Mellen Research University Press, 1992), before my wife and I married, and took the name Newheart, from Ezek 36:26: "A new heart I will give you, and a new spirit I will put within you; and I will remove from your body the heart of stone and give you a heart of flesh."

[2] Walter Wink, *The Bible in Human Transformation: Toward a New Paradigm for Biblical Study* (Philadelphia: Fortress, 1973).

[3] Walter Wink, *Transforming Bible Study: A Leader's Guide* (Nashville: Abingdon, 1980). A revised edition came out in 1989.

biblical criticism is bankrupt. . . . It is bankrupt solely because it is incapable of achieving what most of its practitioners considered its purpose to be: so to interpret the Scriptures that the past becomes alive and illumines our present with new possibilities for personal and social transformation."[4] Wink himself had been personally transformed through seminars at the Guild for Psychological Studies in San Francisco, where the gospels were studied using historical criticism, the Socratic method of question and answer, and the analytical psychology of Carl Jung (the "J" is pronounced like a "Y"), along with art, drama, and movement. In *Transforming Bible Study,* Wink detailed the method he had adapted from the Guild for Psychological Studies and used in leading Bible studies all over the world. I was curious. So eventually I made my pilgrimage to the Guild and participated in a seventeen-day seminar on the Synoptic Gospels at Four Springs, the Guild's conference center north of the Napa Valley. My own wellsprings were fed and stirred. I was deeply touched. Here was a method that could combine the historical and literary analysis I learned in seminary and graduate school, bring it together with psychological insights, and place it in the service of changing lives.[5]

Let me give you an example of how seminar discussions proceeded. Early in the seminar we discussed the baptism of Jesus. We looked at the parallel stories in the Synoptic gospels. A leader asked us about how the accounts differed and which account was likely the earliest. After we discussed these questions we were asked about Jesus' experience of baptism. What might this have meant for him? After further discussion, we were then given art materials and instructed to draw what we thought Jesus' baptism might have meant for him. Though I'm not sure where it is (perhaps my mother's house in Missouri?), I still remember the vivid colors I used in my drawing.

So when I came back from the seminar I began reading Jung, together with friends at the Kansas City Jungian Society. I began leading my classes at Saint Paul School of Theology and Central Baptist Theological Seminary (and later Howard University School of Divinity) in the way I had

---

[4] Wink, *The Bible in Human Transformation,* 1, 2.

[5] See Elizabeth Boyden Howes' Appendix in Wink, *The Bible in Human Transformation,* 84–90, for a list of questions used in the Guild seminars. See also Wink, *Transforming Bible Study,* 121–50, for sample questions he uses in his workshops, which are based on the kinds of questions used at the Guild. A lectionary-based Bible study resource called *The Bible Workbench* presents questions (and space to answer them) in the style of the Guild. This method is set out in William L. Dols, *Awakening the Fire Within: A Primer on Issue-Centered Education* (St. Louis: The Educational Center, 1994). For more information about *The Bible Workbench,* call the Educational Center at 1-800-624-4644.

been taught at the Guild. I did not give up lecturing. (God forbid!) But I did supplement it by asking the students open-ended questions about a particular biblical text, beginning with historical and literary questions and moving to contemporary personal and social questions. Questions usually developed on three ever-deepening levels: What is going on in the text? How is what is going on in the text like what is going on in the world around you? How is what is going on in the text like what is going on in your life?[6] In order to bring creative imagination to critical thinking (and thus a more complete perspective), I led the students to respond to the text, through art, poetry, drama, or movement. For example, just yesterday I had students act out Matthew's story of Jesus walking on the water (14:22-33); two days before, I asked class members to draw their own thorn in the flesh (2 Cor 12:7); and it is not uncommon in my classes for students to write poems or move their bodies to Scripture. Such teaching has been exciting yet difficult, for I have had no real models for teaching this way other than, of course, Wink.

As I began to read Jung, in those days fresh from Four Springs, I also attempted to develop a "Jungian" reading of the gospels, especially the Gospel of John. I did so not just because John was the subject of my dissertation, but also because it seemed most amenable to Jungian interpretation due to its heavy, self-conscious use of symbolism.[7] I also entered into Jungian analysis. I thought that if I was going to apply this stuff to the New Testament, I should first apply it to my own soul. (Scholar, study thyself!)

What was it that captivated me about the psychological interpretation of the New Testament? It took seriously the reality of the unconscious. Historical and narrative criticism had done a good job of addressing the conscious issues of the text but, at least in the forms I was exposed to, they

---

[6] For more about developing these sorts of questions see Dols, *Awakening the Fire Within,* 165–81. These are the types of questions pursued in *The Bible Workbench,* mentioned in the previous note.

[7] See Michael E. Willett, "Jung and John," *Explorations: Journal for Adventurous Thought* (Fall 1988) 77–92; Michael Willett Newheart, "Johannine Symbolism," in David L. Miller, ed., *Jung and the Interpretation of the Bible* (New York: Continuum, 1995) 71–91, reprinted as "The Psychology of Johannine Symbolism," in J. H. Ellens and W. G. Rollins, eds., *Psychology and the Bible: A New Way to Read Scriptures* (Westport, CT: Praeger, forthcoming); idem, "Toward a Psycho-Literary Reading of the Fourth Gospel," in Fernando F. Segovia, ed., *"What is John?": Readers and Readings of the Fourth Gospel.* Society of Biblical Literature Symposium Series 3 (Atlanta: Scholars, 1996) 43–58; idem, "The Soul of the Father and the Son: A Psychological (yet Playful and Poetic) Approach to the Father-Son Language in the Fourth Gospel," *Semeia: Experimental Journal of Biblical Criticism* 85 (1999) 155–75; idem, *Word and Soul: A Psychological, Literary, and Cultural Reading of the Fourth Gospel* Books (Collegeville: The Liturgical Press, 2001).

did not address the whole person, that is, both the conscious and the unconscious. I was a psychology and religion major in college; I had taken a number of pastoral care classes in seminary; and in the later stages of graduate school I was in group counseling. Though none of these experiences was Jungian in orientation, they did take seriously this rather amorphous thing called "the psyche." So it seemed natural that I should turn to psychology for the interpretation of the New Testament. Psychology seemed to help me bring body, mind, and soul together.

So What's "Psychological" About Psychological Biblical Criticism?

What is psychological criticism anyway, at least as it's practiced on the Bible? That question can best be answered by the person who has done more than anyone to put psychological criticism on the biblical studies map, Wayne Rollins. He writes, "The goal of a psychological-critical approach is to examine texts . . . as expressions of the structure, processes, and habits of the human psyche, both in individual and collective manifestations, past and present." He includes in "texts" everything related to their production and reception, including transmission, reading, and interpretation.[8] According to Rollins, then, psychological biblical criticism can be used historically and literarily. To use language used in Chapter 1, it can be used either to look at the text as a "window" or as a "mirror."[9] In other words, psychological biblical critics would be "doing windows" when they described the psyche of a biblical text's author or first hearers/readers, and they would be "cleaning mirrors" when they described the psyche of a text's characters or contemporary hearers/readers.

Psychological biblical criticism is still gaining legitimacy in the eyes of biblical scholars. While narrative criticism began to "take off" in the 1970s, it was not until the 1990s that psychological biblical criticism began to take its place on the biblical critical stage. Two important books were published at the recent "turn of the century" that demonstrated that psychological biblical criticism had finally come of age: *Soul and Psyche: The Bible in Psychological Perspective* by Wayne Rollins, mentioned above as perhaps the father of psychological biblical criticism, and *Psychological Biblical Criticism* by D. Andrew Kille, who was the first person

---

[8] Wayne G. Rollins, *Soul and Psyche: The Bible in Psychological Perspective* (Minneapolis: Fortress, 1999) 77–78. This definition is quoted approvingly in D. Andrew Kille, *Psychological Biblical Criticism*. Guides to Biblical Scholarship: Old Testament Series (Minneapolis: Fortress, 2001) 3.

[9] See above, Chapter 1, 8.

to earn a Ph.D. in psychological biblical criticism. Rollins helpfully sum-marized and analyzed the myriad studies that have been going on in this ever-burgeoning field. Kille, in his book in the prestigious "Guides to Bib-lical Scholarship" series, introduced readers to the method itself (though one might say "methods themselves") by taking one text, the Garden of Eden stories in Genesis 2–3, and looking at it from various psychological perspectives. Finally, after years of alienation we psychological biblical critics were welcome in the garden to eat, along with other scholars, from the tree of knowledge. And there was much "fruitful" discussion. And God saw that it was good.

In many ways psychological biblical criticism carries through the centrality of "story" in narrative criticism. Psychological criticism searches for the "soul stories," or the deep human stories that shape human experience and behavior, both in a text and in reading (or hearing) a text. What "soul stories" illumine Mark's story of the Gerasene demoniac?

In expressing these "soul stories" no one method or theory holds sway. In other words, there is no "one way" to do psychological biblical criticism.[10] The situation is different from that in narrative criticism, where Seymour Chatman's model seems to be "one way" that has proven very popular. Several psychological critical studies, though, have been done from the perspective of the two leading psychodynamic psychologists, Sigmund Freud and Carl Jung, both of whom take seriously the reality of the unconscious. In this chapter we will look at Freudian and Jungian per-spectives on Mark and the Gerasene. In the next chapter we will look at perspectives derived from two theorists who are not often classed as psy-chologists, René Girard and Frantz Fanon. In the final "psychological-critical" chapter I will present my own "soul" reading of the Gerasene.

Sigmund Freud

Just as Albert Einstein transformed our view of science, and Karl Marx our view of economics, Sigmund Freud transformed our view of psy-chology. We simply see ourselves differently than we did prior to his book *The Interpretation of Dreams,* published in 1900. Thanks to him and oth-ers, we are living in a "psychological era," in which it is not uncommon to talk about the unconscious. Indeed, several of Freud's major concepts are part of modern jargon. This was pressed home to me when I attended a rally in the fall of 2002 opposing war against Iraq. I saw a banner that read, "IT'S AN OEDIPAL THING!" The banner was referring to Freud's use of

---

[10] See Kille, *Psychological Biblical Criticism,* 37.

the Oedipus complex, in which he said that the son falls in love with the mother and attempts to kill the father. (I think the protestors were saying that George W. Bush was getting at Saddam Hussein because his father failed to do so. The younger Bush would therefore "kill" his father and win the affections of his mother.) Furthermore, we often hear of "Freudian slips," when a speaker unintentionally says something that gives away his or her unconscious intentions.

In some ways, though, Freud is out of fashion. College psychology texts rarely deal extensively with his theories. He is not read in many graduate psychology programs. Few people can afford the time and money of several sessions of psychoanalysis each week, and health insurance organizations often do not pay for it. Yet at the academic level people are still interested in Freud; indeed, he is making something of a comeback in intellectual circles. Psychoanalytic literary criticism analyzes literature from a Freudian (and post-Freudian perspective).[11] It is interesting to note that *The Postmodern Bible*, which deals with various forms of contemporary biblical criticism, includes a chapter on psychoanalytic criticism, but no other forms of psychological criticism.[12] It may seem strange to use Freud in biblical interpretation, because he did not often deal with the Bible and he was quite antagonistic to religion, calling it a "universal obsessional neurosis" (though he modified that position in later life).[13]

Freudian theory has nevertheless proven helpful to some psychological biblical critics. I will not attempt a summary of Freudian thought, for basic introductions to Freud are widely available.[14] Rather, I want to point to the "soul stories" of psychoanalysis and then look at how those stories have been helpful to psychological biblical critics in interpreting the story of the Gerasene.

1. Freud's Stories of the Unconscious

Freud understood that consciousness was merely the tip of the iceberg and that much of mental life was determined by the unconscious. To speak about the relationship of consciousness to the unconscious, Freud pro-

---

[11] See Shoshana Felman, ed., *Literature and Psychoanalysis: The Question of Reading: Otherwise* (Baltimore: Johns Hopkins University Press, 1982).

[12] The Bible and Culture Collective, *The Postmodern Bible* (New Haven: Yale University Press, 1995) 187–224.

[13] See Rollins, *Soul and Psyche,* 33–46 for a discussion of Freud and the Bible.

[14] For brief introductions to Freud see Michael Kahn, *Basic Freud: Psychoanalytic Thought for the 21st Century* (New York: Basic Books, 2002); Anthony Storr, *Freud. Past Masters* (Oxford: Oxford University Press, 1989).

posed the id, the ego, and the superego. The id consists of all our unconscious drives and instincts. It operates on the basis of what Freud called the pleasure principle. The superego is our conscience, which consists of the rules and prohibitions of parents and society. It is partly conscious but mostly unconscious. Negotiating between these two, as well as the outside world, is the ego, our executive function that operates on the basis of what Freud called the reality principle.

When we are infants we are utterly under the sway of the id. We respond completely to our drives and desires. We are under control of the pleasure principle. Furthermore, we consider ourselves the center of the universe. Everyone and everything exists to serve our interests. Each of us, then, in the beginning, is "His or Her Majesty the Baby." As our ego begins to develop, however, we begin to operate according to the reality principle and to repress certain feelings. What is repressed, however, does not disappear. Rather, it emerges in dreams (what Freud called the royal road to the unconscious), neuroses (i.e., self-destructive behavior), and "parapraxes" (i.e., slips of the tongue and of the pen and certain forgetting and errors).

A central story in the unconscious for Freud is the Oedipus complex, from the Greek legend of King Oedipus, portrayed in Sophocles' drama, who unknowingly kills his father and marries his mother. Freud claimed that all children unconsciously desire to get rid of their same-sex parent and be the lover of their opposite-sex parent. Freud maintained that how one resolves the Oedipus complex is crucial for one's identity and one's relationship with men and women, not the least of which is one's spouse.

A third Freudian story is that the human psyche is locked in a struggle between *Eros* (sexual love) and *Thanatos* (death). *Eros* is the life energy, which strives to create and bring new things into being, thus moving us forward. *Thanatos*, however, is the death instinct, which seeks to destroy and bring us back to the original state of being. It takes in our aggressiveness and destructiveness. Freud maintained that these two instincts are always struggling against one another in the psyche of the individual.

Finally, Freud maintains that a child develops language in order to express desire. Freud observed his eighteen-month-old grandson using language to compensate for his absent mother. He threw a spool attached to a string over the side of the bed and said, "Ooh," which Freud understood as "fort," German for "gone" or "away." He reeled the toy in and said, "A," which to Freud was "da," "there" in English. Freud contends that the child was learning to cope with his mother's absence by substituting the spool and thereby learning how to use language to express his desire. Freud's disciple Jacques Lacan has further explored the link between language and the unconscious, which he believes are always bound together. Indeed,

Lacan said that "the unconscious is structured like a language."[15] Language is the first tool of repression, and the unconscious always tries to find a loophole in language that allows for pleasure. This holds true for all the ways we process language, including speaking, listening, writing, and reading. As Petri Merenlahti writes in his summary of Lacan, "We read not only for discipline but also for pleasure."[16]

These are the stories that are foundational to psychoanalysis: the unconscious, the Oedipus complex, *Eros* and *Thanatos,* and language as expressive of desire. Others could be added, for psychoanalysis is a vast enterprise. But now we turn to how psychological biblical critics have used these stories to interpret the Gerasene story.

2. Uleyn's "Uncanny" Reading

I am aware of only one extended psychoanalytic reading of the Gerasene story, and it is simply entitled "The Possessed Man of Gerasa (Marc [sic] 5.1-20): A Psychoanalytic Interpretation of Reader-reactions," by Arnold Uleyn.[17] He uses the psychoanalytic category of "the uncanny," which he says this story evokes in readers. He writes, "As a technical term, in the psychoanalytic sense, the Uncanny . . . is a feeling of being upset and scared by something that appears as strange, disturbing or even as horrific, whereas it is in fact something that long ago has been very familiar and near."[18] An uncanny experience, then, alerts us to the return of the repressed. In reading the Gospel of Mark we identify with the hero Jesus because, in Uleyn's words, "he activates our narcissistic and oedipal wishes by indulging forbidden impulses and behavior."[19] Jesus is omnipotent; he heals people, banishes evil spirits, and defies religious authorities. He has the sort of power for which we long. By identifying with him we experience vicariously that same sort of power we felt in infancy. Reading, then, is a return to the cradle, which was our throne.

I would take Uleyn one step further. He says at the beginning of his essay that we experience uncanny feelings when faced with two categories

---

[15] Quoted in The Bible and Culture Collective, *The Postmodern Bible,* 198.

[16] Petri Merenlahti, "Reading Mark for the Pleasure of Fantasy," in Ellens and Rollins, eds., *Psychology and the Bible: A New Way to Read Scriptures* (forthcoming).

[17] A.J.R. Uleyn, "The Possessed Man of Gerasa: A Psychoanalytic Interpretation of Reader Reactions," in J. van Belzen and Jan van der Lans, eds., *Current Issues in Psychology of Religion: Proceedings of the Third Symposium on the Psychology of Religion in Europe* (Amsterdam: Rodopi, 1986) 90–96.

[18] Ibid. 91.

[19] Ibid. 93. Here he is building on his earlier article, "A Psychoanalytic Approach to Mark's Gospel," *Lumen Vitae* 32 (1977) 479–93.

of persons: the very disturbed and those who have superhuman capacities. Uleyn notes that this story features both figures, but he emphasizes our identification with the man who has superhuman capacities, Jesus. He seems to neglect the fact we also identify with the "very disturbed one," the demoniac. Like Jesus, he too is strong, smashing the chains that bind him. He allows us to return to the cradle too, to indulge our fantasies of omnipotence. The two strong men meet, and the stronger casts out the strong. So there is a way to control the seemingly uncontrollable. One can be benevolently omnipotent over one's feelings of malevolent omnipotence! What a satisfying story!

Or is it? After his act of omnipotence over great evil, the Gerasenes chase Jesus away. Even omnipotence has its limits. Indeed, it leads to disenchantment, according to Uleyn. Mark evokes the illusion of omnipotence and undermines it. He evokes it in that he depicts Jesus doing what adults cannot do. "He indulges the unrepressed infantile immoral desires through rebellious acts, which are denials of the rational."[20] Yet Jesus is rejected, here by the Gerasenes and later by the scribes and chief priests and even by his own disciples. Uleyn calls this story "a forewarning" of the end when Jesus is "completely powerless." He says that the Gerasene story is the first red light. It is the "anticipation of later total disenchantment."[21] In the end, are our feelings of omnipotence at least partly indulged through the promise of resurrection?" But it is only promise, unfulfilled promise, with fearful women and scattered disciples squelching proclamations of vindication.

3. Listening to Legion's Language

Martha Burdette, in a brief essay in a volume that compares the Gerasene narrative and Margaret Atwood's story "The Sin Eater," applies Freud's insight about language and desire to the Markan story in one pregnant paragraph.[23] She notes that the Gerasene's sanity is restored through language. He babbles incoherently in the graveyard, but he runs and calls Jesus by name, leading Jesus to ask him his name and then transfer the

[20] Uleyn, "The Possessed Man of Gerasa," 95.

[21] Ibid.

[22] In his earlier article, "A Psychoanalytic Approach to Mark's Gospel," Uleyn does speak about faith in the resurrection as "a fantasy of immortality" and "the regressive-progressive fantasy of a permanent union with God" (491–92).

[23] Martha Burdette, "Sin Eating and Sin Making," in Robert Detweiler and William G. Doty, eds., *The Daemonic Imagination*. American Academy of Religion Studies in Religion 60 (Atlanta: Scholars, 1990) 161.

demons to the pigs. Healed by Jesus' words, he wants to follow Jesus, but is instead left with words, which he is to tell others. "This story of the transference of sin onto the swine, also considered unclean, prepares the Gerasene's audience and others for a later story of transference. The transference of humankind's sins to Christ will be the narrative that all believers will be instructed to repeat to others."[24]

Petri Merenlahti presents a Lacanian reading of the gospel in his essay "Reading Mark for the Pleasure of Fantasy," in which he focuses on the reader's unconscious pleasure-driven side.[25] He calls Mark "a fantastic gospel." He says that fantasy links the text with the unconscious and makes it pleasurable. In what ways is the reading of the Gerasene story pleasurable? Merenlahti does not deal specifically with this passage, though we have discussed it in personal conversation and via e-mail. He does note in his essay that the first-century Mediterranean world had a "one-sex model of humanity," in that the female body was looked upon as an incomplete version of the male body. Merenlahti goes on to say that manliness was in a constant state of crisis, as men lived in "a culture of castration anxiety." One might say, then, that the Gerasene attempts to revolt against convention, against the rule of the father, in Lacan's terms, "the name of the father." The Gerasenes, however, try to bind him so that he won't challenge the father. In other words, they try to "feminize" him. But the Gerasene attempts to feminize himself through his self-stoning, which is his attempt at castration. He deals with castration anxiety by attempting to castrate himself! Jesus feminizes the Gerasene too, but in a different way. He binds the strong man Satan (feminizing him too?) and casts out the demons so that the Gerasene is able to accept the name of the father, who for Jesus is God the Father. Indeed, this serves as a lesson to the disciples, who want to overthrow the Father's rule.

I will append here my own "erotic/thanatotic" (lovely/deadly) pseudo-psychoanalytic reading. I find and I feel much *Eros* and much *Thanatos* in this passage. There is Jesus, who desires, who longs to go to the other side, a longing that is not dampened even by the raging storm, but rather calms the storm. There is Legion, who is *Thanatos* incarnate, living in the graveyard and attempting to kill (castrate!) what little *Eros* lies within him. But that little *Eros* carries him to Jesus, whom he accuses of wanting to be like the Gerasenes and torment—indeed, kill—him. Jesus, however, extends his desire to this raging man, just as he extended it to the raging sea: Jesus asks the demoniac's name and casts out his demons—

[24] Ibid.
[25] Merenlahti, "Reading Mark."

into pigs, who rush to their death in the sea. The Gerasenes, who are possessed by death, do not desire this divine demon-exorcizing desire, and they send Jesus away. The man loves Jesus and desires to be with him. No, Jesus says. Go home and tell about the Lord's mercy, about God's desire, God's *Eros* that has overcome *Thanatos,* the death that had so encompassed him. It is not Jesus' desire that has brought him across the sea and cast out the demons, but it is God's desire. Go and tell. He does, but not at home and not about God. Instead, he preaches in the Ten Cities about Jesus. He tells the story of desire, his and Jesus', and the people are amazed. Perhaps their desire is awakened, too. I know that mine is.

Freud enables us to see the "unconscious" of this passage. We see that this story allows the repressed to return, shows the power of language in expressing desire, and expresses the struggle between *Eros* and *Thanatos.*

But I'm conscious that we have more to say about the unconscious.

Carl Jung

Jung is also a psychologist of the unconscious. Both Freud and Jung are "psychodynamic" theorists, while Freud is "psychoanalytic" and Jung is "analytical." Indeed, Jung was Freud's heir-apparent until he "went astray." Jung went from Freudian heir to Freudian heretic because, among other things, he accepted the benefits of religion to psychological functioning. Many people today use Jungian language as a resource for spiritual growth. Compared with Freud, then, Jung would seem more amenable to a biblical interpretation, not only because he was positively disposed to religion, but because his writings are littered to references to the Bible.[26] In fact, Jung is popular not only among religious people, but also in the public at large. We often hear Jungian terms like "introvert and extrovert," "archetype," "shadow side," and "individuation."

So let us now consider Jung's foundational stories, especially as they compare to Freud's. Then we will look at how those stories help illuminate the Gerasene story.

1. Jung's Story of the Unconscious

With Freud, Jung accepted the reality of the unconscious, but he made a distinction between the personal unconscious and the collective unconscious. The personal is essentially what Freud referred to when he spoke of

---

[26] See Rollins, *Soul and Psyche,* 46–59 for a discussion of Jung and the Bible. Also see his *Jung and the Bible* (Atlanta: John Knox, 1983).

the unconscious. The collective unconscious, however, is Jung's own term. It is that which we share with all people around the globe. In other words, we have our own personal wells that all connect to one large source of water.

Within the unconscious, both personal and collective, are certain tendencies called "archetypes." In his helpful introduction to Jung's thought, Murray Stein defines archetype this way: "An innate potential pattern of imagination, thought, or behavior that can be found among human being[s] in all times and places."[27] Archetypes function in the psyche as instincts do in the body. They produce images that appear in individuals' dreams and in cultural products such as fairy tales, myths, and religious symbols. Three archetypes are the shadow, the anima or animus, and the Self. First, the shadow, which is sometimes referred to as "the dark side," includes everything one refuses to acknowledge about oneself. What is repressed goes into the shadow. Second, anima and animus are the contrasexual aspects of a person. Anima is the feminine element in the man, and animus is the masculine element in the woman. Third, the Self is the archetype of wholeness. It brings together consciousness and the unconscious. It moves one along to individuation, or self-realization.

Archetypal images appear not only in dreams, but also in projections. Jung picked up the idea of projection from Freud but gave it his own twist. We project (i.e., "externalize") our shadow onto others. What we dislike in others is often an indicator of what we dislike in ourselves. (African-Americans have often been the recipients of European-Americans' shadow.) We also project the anima or animus onto members of the opposite sex, often leading to romantic love. We project the Self onto people and symbols in order to progress toward individuation.

In moving down that road, the ego, the center of consciousness, must be alert to the archetypal images and therefore be in dialogue with the unconscious. It must not identify itself too closely with the *persona,* which is the "face" the ego puts on for the world. (The *persona* is in consciousness what the shadow is in the unconscious.) Rather, the ego must establish a strong connection with the Self, thus creating the "ego-self axis," which helps move the person toward individuation. Within the world's religious traditions, for which Jung had great respect, Jesus and the Buddha are symbols of the Self.

Dream interpretation is an important feature of Jungian therapy, even more so now than for Freudians. We look for the archetypal images. For

---

[27] Murray Stein, *Jung's Map of the Soul: An Introduction* (Chicago: Open Court, 1998) 233. Another good introduction to Jung is Jolande Jacobi, *The Psychology of C. G. Jung* (New Haven: Yale University Press, 1973).

example, a woman in the dream of a man often is an anima figure, and a man in the dream of a woman often is an animus figure. The dream is compensating for some attitude in consciousness. The goal, then, is to be in touch with both masculine and feminine in oneself. Similarly, if one dreams about a same-sex figure that seems distasteful or even evil, then that is probably a shadow figure. One needs to be in contact with one's shadow to move toward individuation. Jung also encouraged people to "dream the dream onward" through active imagination exercises, such as art, drama, or poetry.

We also become conscious of the unconscious through becoming aware of our projections. We can withdraw the projection, thereby becoming more conscious and seeing the other as a person. For example, I may be quite upset about a young man I consider lazy. He doesn't get his work done; he seems careless about what he does get done; he doesn't seem to be trying. (These are certainly features European-Americans have projected onto African-Americans! I often catch myself doing this!) I realize, however, that it is difficult for me to relax, that I have unreasonably high expectations for myself, that I am a bit compulsive in what I do. I use this new awareness to do some self-assessment. What is the role of laziness (or relaxation?) in my life? To what extent am I "projecting laziness" onto this young man? How have I repressed "laziness" to meet the demands of my *persona*? How might I recover it and move toward individuation? As I consider such questions I become more conscious and I am able to see the young man more as a person.

So Jung has his own stories to tell about the unconscious. He speaks of both the personal and collective unconscious, of the shadow, self, and anima/animus. One becomes conscious of unconscious content through dreams and projections.

How might these stories help us understand the Gerasene?

2. Legion as Shadow Figure

Diarmuid McGann gives an extended Jungian reading of Mark in his book *The Journeying Self: The Gospel of Mark through a Jungian Perspective*.[28] McGann writes, "Scripture is essential to understanding who we are as a people, and who I am as a person and as an individual."[29] He

---

[28] Diarmuid McGann, *The Journeying Self: The Gospel of Mark Through a Jungian Perspective* (New York: Paulist, 1985). McGann had a followup book on John, *Journeying Within Transcendence: The Gospel of John Through a Jungian Perspective* (New York: Paulist, 1988).

[29] McGann, *The Journeying Self,* 9.

considers the gospel not just as a story of Jesus but as "a story of me, of who I am and who I am becoming."[30] McGann, then, uses Jungian psychology to relate Mark to a person's inner journey. Furthermore, he attempts to approach the text "meditatively," reading it slowly so as to allow it to awaken deeper levels of himself.

McGann meditatively moves through the gospel section by section, viewing each part as a "story of the self." He treats the Gerasene in a chapter entitled "The Shadow."[31] For McGann, Legion is a shadow figure. In order to set up that discussion, though, he talks about Jesus crossing the lake and thereby bringing both sides into union. He says that in our own psyches we must bring together the opposites, such as *persona* and shadow. We project our shadow onto other people, he continues. We must withdraw our projections and integrate our shadow. "The shadow figure comes as a messenger of the unconscious inviting us to pay attention to something bigger than our little ego concerns. The shadow leads us to ourselves, to the deeper self, if we listen attentively."[32]

McGann spotlights the pigs in the story. Using the work of mythologist Joseph Campbell, he notes that across cultures the "sacrificial pig has great significance in terms of birth and death, departure, initiation and return. It relates to the great themes of and frames the moments of the merging of the two worlds of Eternity and Time, death and life, father and son."[33] McGann then suggests that the Gerasene story is touching on the collective unconscious, and we may have what Jung calls "a big dream," that is, a narrative that comes not from the personal unconscious but from the collective unconscious and is therefore fraught with significance.

As he does with each section of the gospel, McGann asks what this story says about the story of the self. He has two points. First, he encourages us to look at our own bodies. They are indicative of disorder or order. They tell us of "our drivenness, our compulsiveness, our destructiveness, our anxiety, etc."[34] The Gerasene was certainly living a disordered bodily existence, as he was living among the tombs and gashing himself. What does my body tell me about myself? "I need to see and feel, and accept the statement that my body is making. Is my body reflecting my conscious life project or is it saying something else that I do not wish to hear but need to hear?"[35] Second, he also asks us to discover the "pigs" in our own lives.

---

[30] Ibid.
[31] Ibid. 71–80.
[32] Ibid. 74.
[33] Ibid. 76.
[34] Ibid. 78.
[35] Ibid. 78–79.

Where do we project our shadow? He writes, "Under the guidance of the self we are called to recognize the shadow and bring it into the light, to integrate its energies, its values, its strength into our personality, to bring them into our conscious mode of operation and grow into the person we are called to become."[36]

3. "Me and My Shadow"

I am attracted to this idea of reading the story meditatively in a Jungian mode. Can I read the text as a story of myself? Can I give myself over to the text so that it can transform me? I will try.

I see Jesus and the disciples land after crossing the Sea of Galilee. The disciples still look a little shaky from their trip. And what a trip it was. The wind was howling, the waves were crashing—and Jesus was asleep! This story speaks to me at an unconscious level, for I know such periods in my life, in my psyche, when I seem all stirred up, all nervous, all anxious, and those thoughts or feelings or practices that are supposed to help me are of no avail. Jesus seems asleep. I cannot connect with the center, with the self. Yet I can wake it up if I wake up, that is, if I become aware of what is being kicked up in my unconscious by circumstances around me. What am I projecting onto people, onto events? Eventually I find my center, which wakes (me) up and says, "Peace, be still." And there is great calm.

The disciples, however, don't share that calm. The calming of the sea was the unsettling of the disciples, for they were afraid and asked, "Who is this, that wind and sea obey him?" I know! I know! It is the Spirit-endowed Son of God, who both stirs and calms me.

So Jesus and the disciples come to the other side of the sea, to the region of the Gerasenes. Huh? Gerasa is over thirty miles from the sea. How could the region of the Gerasenes be on the other side of the sea from Galilee? This detail as well as others (e.g. the pigs rushing off a cliff into the sea) makes the story seem almost like a dream, for reality is a little skewed here. I will interpret it as I would a dream.

Once they reach shore, Jesus gets out of the boat, leaving these uncomprehending disciples behind. But he is not alone for long, for some madman comes rushing up to him. He is naked and bloody and wild-eyed. He screams! He repulses me; he attracts me. He moves me deeply. Oh God, who is this creature? He is me, my shadow figure. I hear his cries as he gashes, slashes, and mashes his own flesh. Ugh! I think of my own self-destructive behavior. I, too, wound myself with messages of self-hatred.

---

[36] Ibid. 80.

But I have not gone mad as he has. I have not given my ego over to forces of the unconscious as he has.

I'm particularly struck with his rage, HIS RAGE! He is the man I fear I will become if I give vent to my rage. I fear that people will come and bind me. So I stuff my rage. I can't express it. People will stone me. So I stone myself. I am dead. I cut off that part of me. But I am strong with this rage, this passion, this woundedness, all of which seem to know no bounds. It also knows no bonds! Or rather, it knows the bonds I try to put on myself, which I keep breaking. So, like the Gerasene, I live among the dead.

The demoniac, however, is alive enough to come to see Jesus. He knows that Jesus has numinous power, power to transform. I know that too, for I have seen the calming of the sea. He falls down before Jesus. What was that he said? Was it his name? LEGION. Many. Many demons. Many devilish troops occupying his soul while devilish troops occupy the land. The oppressors have driven him mad. I think of my own oppressors. I have accepted their messages (their chains and fetters) that I am somehow inadequate, somehow unclean, and it has driven me crazy! The demoniac carries my craziness resulting from my rage at the powers and my fear to confront the powers.

The demons want to stay in the land, so they plead with Jesus to send them into the pigs. The pigs, yes, pigs! I think of the authority figures (parents, pastors, administrators) who have attempted to bind and stone me. (Is it upon them that I project my shadow? How have I oppressed people?) So the demons go into the pigs, and the pigs go into the sea. Yes! Yes! So I have my catharsis, cheering the death of the oppressors.

So the man now sits, dressed and sane. SANE. Released from his demons. I see him there so satisfied, so contented, and so not tortured! It is what I long for, to be delivered from my own torture, my own binding, my own demons.

The Gerasenes are not nearly so pleased; indeed, they are afraid, just like the disciples in the boat. Yes, I know that feeling too, that resistance to transformation, because transformation is scary. Better to keep my projections in place, better to live unconsciously than to withdraw the projections and come to consciousness.

The people chase Jesus off, and Jesus chases the healed man off—so that he can tell what has happened to him. He does that, all over the region, and his hearers are amazed. I can believe that. What an amazing story, one that stirs the depths! And it keeps on stirring, as I reflect on the issues that have been kicked up for me: the "possession" that results when I allow my

anxiety to squash my anger, and my projection of my shadow onto authority figures. I, too, am amazed.

A Jungian reading of this passage helps us appreciate the Gerasene as
a shadow figure. We are attracted to this passage because of the great
strength of the unacknowledged unconscious. We know this in our lives.
We must be sensitive to dreams, to projections, and to literature to see
where the shadow is attempting to erupt in our lives.

Conclusion

Freud and Jung point us to the unconscious dynamics of a text.
Freudians lift up the Oedipus conflict and the return of the repressed, for
example, while Jungians highlight the archetypes, such as shadow and
Self. As we are in touch with these unconscious dynamics, we grow in psychological and emotional maturity.

Both Freud and Jung speak about looking at a text as a dream. I am
mindful of two dreams I had on consecutive nights in December 2003,
when I was working intensively on this book. In the first dream I held a
baby in my arms. It was my baby. It was not clear whether it was a boy or
a girl. I was at the house where we used to live in Washington, D.C. The
baby looked out into the hallway. I was not sure what it was looking at. The
baby was quite young. It had something on its head. It looked toward me. I
was surprised at how much older it looked. It had big dark brown eyes and
dark hair. The second dream was quite brief. A violent man came out of the
wall from a carving. He had killed someone.

These two dreams dramatically pick up aspects of the Gerasene story.
The demoniac is a violent man, attempting to kill someone: himself. He
has a new birth, however, as the demons are expelled from him. Is there a
new birth in me as I work with this story? Yes, if I keep in mind that within
me is a violent, murderous man who has killed, is killing me.

These psychodynamic readings are quite insightful, but we might
raise questions. Are Freud's and Jung's readings too individualistic (i.e.,
too male, too Western)? Do they fail to take sufficient account of the social
setting, both the social setting of the story and the social setting of the
reader-hearer of the story? Hmm.

Provocative questions, huh? Don't stop to think about them too long,
though. Keep on reading!

CHAPTER FIVE

Legion Scapegoated and (De)Colonized: Girard and Fanon

Girard and Fanon? You might be thinking, "Who are they? I heard about Freud and Jung in psychology class, but not Girard or Fanon." Alas, they are usually not mentioned in psychology texts. Girard is becoming popular among a wide range of scholars who are interested in a new field often dubbed "conflict studies," and Fanon is better known in postcolonial studies than in psychology or biblical studies. As in the previous chapter, we will attempt to explicate the foundational stories of their theories and show how biblical scholars have used those stories in interpreting the Gerasene stories.

René Girard

I said in the introduction to the book that I am a Quaker, that is, a member of the Religious Society of Friends, who have been, as the society's website says, "religious witnesses to peace since 1660."[1] Though I have been attending Quaker worship only since the late 1990s, I have been associated with the peace movement since the late 1970s. As a biblical scholar interested in peace and justice, therefore, I yearned to find some critical tools that would help me get an intellectual handle on violence (and nonviolence) in the biblical tradition. I think that I have found such a handle with the theories of René Girard.

---

[1] "The Religious Society of Friends," n. p. 31 January 2004. Available: http://www.quaker.org.

I had first heard of Girard over a decade ago through Walter Wink's trilogy on the Powers in the New Testament,[2] though at that time Girard just didn't "take." A few years ago, however, my friend and colleague Ron Hopson, associate professor of psychology of religion at Howard Divinity School, said that he was interested in Girard, and he recommended Gil Bailie's book as a good introduction to Girard and the application of his thought to the biblical tradition.[3] I read the book—devoured it, actually. I was interested, I was intrigued, and I was deeply moved. So, more about Girard would I know! I later discovered that a lot of folks are interested in Girard, as shown by the Colloquium on Violence and Religion (COV&R), an international organization founded to discuss Girard's thought and its relevance to contemporary religious violence.[4] Another colleague and friend, Kwasi Kwakye-Nwako, assistant professor of world religions at Howard, has also explored Girard's thought to help him understand violence in the various religious traditions. So we are the Girardian three (trio, trinity, triumvirate—hmm, "three" or "trio" will do well, thank you).

I will summarize the foundational stories of Girard's theory, describe his approach to the Gerasene, and point to two biblical scholars who use his work in interpreting the Gerasene.

1 Girard's "Mimetic" Story

René Girard is a French literary critic who has recently retired from Stanford University. (Indeed, of the four primary psychological theorists discussed in Chapters 4 and 5 of this book, he is the only one who is still alive!) His thought is used in literature, anthropology, psychology, and religious studies. Just as we looked at the key stories of Freud and Jung, so we

[2] In his second volume on the Powers, Wink uses Girard for his interpretation of the Gerasene. See below, 76–77. He also discusses Girard in the seventh chapter of his third volume, entitled "Breaking the Spiral of Violence: The Power of the Cross," *Engaging the Powers: Discernment and Resistance in a World of Domination* (Minneapolis: Fortress, 1992) 139–55.

[3] Gil Bailie, *Violence Unveiled: Humanity at the Crossroads* (New York: Crossroad, 1995). I have also found helpful James G. Williams, *The Bible, Violence, and the Sacred: Liberation from the Myth of Sanctioned Violence* (New York: HarperCollins, 1991). A clear, brief summary of Girardian thought is found in Mack C. Stirling, "Violent Religion: René Girard's Theory of Culture," in J. Harold Ellens, ed., *The Destructive Power of Religion: Violence in Judaism, Christianity, and Islam* (Westport, CT: Praeger, 2004) 2:11–50. My summary is much indebted to Stirling's. Another useful essay in that book is Cheryl McGuire, "Judaism, Christianity, and Girard: The Violent Messiahs," 51–84, which includes an extensive annotated bibliography.

[4] See their website http://theol.uibk.ac.at/cover/.

will approach Girard. His story can be summed up in a single word: *mimesis*, that is, imitation. "Mimesis" and its related words "mimeticism" and especially "mimetic" are strewn all over the works of Girard and his followers. There is mimetic desire, mimetic rivalry, and mimetic crisis. (Girardian thought is often called "mimetic theory.") But not only are there things mimetic, there is also the scapegoat. So let us mine the mimetic to see what riches lie there.

Since we spent much of the last chapter discussing Freud (and his heir/heretic Jung), it would be helpful to begin by comparing Girard with Freud, for the two look at "desire" differently. For Girard, desire is "mimetic," that is, imitative. We desire certain things because others have them. As Girard writes, "Desire chooses its objects through the mediation of a model."[5] For Freud, desire is primarily sexual, and it is the son's desire for his mother, which arises spontaneously and brings him into conflict with his father. Thus results the Oedipus complex, which we discussed in the previous chapter. Girard, however, maintains that the son desires the mother because he is imitating the father. The Oedipal complex, then, is not central for Girard as it is for Freud. In other words, for Girard desire is interpersonal (between persons), while for Freud it is intrapersonal (within the individual).[6]

Stirling, in his excellent summary of Girard, talks about the "triangular structure of desire" in which the subject, or the self, is first in relationship to the other, who is the model or mediator. The subject desires an object because the model possesses that object.[7] In a memorable analogy, Gil Bailie notes that a young child will not be playing with a certain toy, but then a second child comes and starts playing with that toy, and the first child suddenly starts wanting that toy.[8] "Mine!" Conflict results. Mimetic desire becomes mimetic rivalry, which is a "nearly ubiquitous feature of human relations."[9] Mimetic rivals blame one another. Children struggling over a toy will both say, "S/he took (or is trying to take) my toy!" The rivals become doubles of one another, saying the same words and doing the same things. And they often become violent with one another. Stirling maintains that this violence can be directed in three possible directions: toward the model (murder), toward the self (suicide, insanity, or submission), or toward an arbitrary third entity (scapegoat).[10]

---

[5] Cited in Sterling, "Violent Religion," 14.

[6] I am indebted to my colleague Ron Hopson for this insight and wording.

[7] Stirling, "Violent Religion," 12–14.

[8] Bailie, *Violence Unveiled*, 116–18.

[9] Stirling, "Violent Religion," 18.

[10] Ibid. 21.

Just as all of us are involved in mimetic rivalries, we are all involved in scapegoating. Whenever we have a bad day at work or school, we often take it out at home, or vice-versa. Racial prejudice is an example of scapegoating, in which one racial or ethnic group is singled out as a "menace to society." Because of the legacy of slavery, African-Americans have often served as scapegoats in our society, being victims of lynching, discrimination, and segregation. Yet other racial groups, such as Native Americans, Hispanic Americans, and Asian Americans, have all been victims of scapegoating violence. In the post-9/11 world Muslims and other non-Christians have been scapegoated. Indeed, anyone who is "different" as defined by majority culture (the homeless, the mentally ill, homosexuals, bisexuals, etc.) is scapegoated.

The scapegoat is innocent of the collective guilt a group assigns to it. The group projects its sins, evil, and guilt onto the scapegoat, and then it commits violence against the scapegoat, resulting in healing and peace for the group. Indeed, these feelings are said to come from the scapegoat, who is now perceived as a powerful god. Girard speaks about the "double transference" in which violence is first projected onto the scapegoat but then both violence and peace are perceived to come from the scapegoat. This scapegoat-god is "bivalent," that is, both good and bad. For example, African-Americans are often scapegoated as violent, criminal, and sexual, yet African American cultural expressions such as jazz, hip-hop fashions, and soul food pervade American life.

The scapegoat generates culture and religion. Indeed, Girard maintains that religion is the fundamental institution of culture. Religion, in turn, generates ritual, prohibition, and myth. Ritual reenacts the mimetic crisis and its resolution. Prohibition warns against behavior that would lead to another mimetic crisis. Myth tells the story of the original murder, exonerating the murderers and blaming the victim.

Girard maintains a sharp distinction between the Bible and myth. Indeed, the Bible unveils the scapegoating tendency that myth seeks to sacralize. According to the Bible, God takes the side of the victims, as shown primarily at the cross. For Girard, Jesus' death is not a ritual sacrifice required by the Father. Rather, it is Jesus' voluntary giving up of his life in order to expose the scapegoating mechanism of the world. Stirling writes, "Jesus suffered himself to become 'scapegoat for the world' in order to get us to renounce all scapegoating."[11] In the life of Jesus Christ, God is revealed as loving and nonviolent.

---

[11] Ibid. 46.

Girard argues, then, that humanity's central story is that of mimetic rivalry, which often results in scapegoating. How is that relevant to the Gerasene story?

2. Girard's Mimetic Gerasenes

Not only is Girard the only living theorist we are dealing with, he is also the only one who has written an essay specifically on the Gerasene. It appears in his book *The Scapegoat,* in which he discusses a number of passages in the gospels, such as Peter's denial, the execution of John the Baptist, and the Passion narratives. The essay on the Gerasene constitutes Chapter 13 of the book and is entitled, "The Demons of Gerasa."[12] He begins by saying that mimeticism, through the mediation of the scapegoat, is the source of all order and disorder. He continues that the gospels do not contain myth, for myth maintains that the victim is guilty and the gospels insist on the innocence of the victim. Girard writes, "By revealing that [scapegoat] mechanism and the surrounding mimeticism, the Gospels set in motion the only textual mechanism that can put an end to humanity's imprisonment in the system of mythological representation based on the false transcendence of a victim who is made sacred because of the unanimous verdict of guilt."[13] So it is the Gospel vs. Myth. Myth accuses the victim, while the Gospel exonerates the victim.

Girard says that when the "false transcendence" appears in its unity (in both order and disorder), the gospels call it "Satan," but when it appears in its multiplicity (in which disorder predominates), the gospels refer to demons. Girard then turns his gaze to the Gerasene, the longest of the stories of Jesus casting out demons. He notes how the demoniac is both dead and alive, both bound and free. His situation is the result of the "mimetic crisis that leads to loss of differentiation and to persecution."[14] He notes how the Gerasenes and the demoniac are caught up in a kind of "cyclical pathology" in which the people repeatedly go out to bind the demoniac, even though he always breaks the bonds. They are participating in ritual, behaving "like sick men whose every action fosters rather than decreases the disease."[15] Girard maintains that the Gerasenes benefit from their participation in this ritual because they beg Jesus to leave when he disrupts the cycle.

---

[12] René Girard, *The Scapegoat,* trans. Yvonne Freccero (Baltimore: The Johns Hopkins University Press, 1986) 165–83.

[13] Ibid. 166.

[14] Ibid.

[15] Ibid. 169.

Girard takes up Jean Starobinski's term "autolapidation," self-ston-ing, and notes its "mimetic character."[16] The demoniac fears he will be ex-pelled and stoned, so he expels and stones himself. Girard points to the "reciprocal relationship" of this mimetic rivalry. "The possessed imitates these Gerasenes who stone their victims, but the Gerasenes in return imi-tate the possessed."[17] (Matthew, Girard notes, literalizes the doubling by presenting two demoniacs.)

Girard also points out how attached the Gerasenes and the demons are to one another. The demons do not want to leave the region, but when they do, through the drowning of the demon-possessed pigs, the Gerasenes want Jesus to leave. The demons, the demoniac, and the Gerasenes participate in a violent psychopathological relationship, in which one cannot do without the other. Girard notes that the pigs' running off a cliff, like the demoniac stoning himself, has "collective, ritual, and penal connotations,"[18] for ston-ing and casting off a cliff were two widespread ritualistic methods of execu-tion in ancient societies. Here, however, it is not the victim that goes over the cliff while the crowd watches, but the crowd (of demons) that goes over the cliff while the victim watches! Girard writes, "The miracle of Gerasa re-verses the universal schema of violence fundamental to all societies of the world."[19] So the exorcism of the demoniac and the drowning of the demons threaten the system in which the Gerasenes have grown comfortable. Girard shows how the demons are more reasonable than the humans. They try to negotiate with Jesus, but their worst fears are realized, for by drowning they are "sent out of the region," which they begged not to have happen.

The demoniac is possessed not just by the demons but by the Gerasenes themselves. "The demons are in the image of the human group; they are the *imago* of this group because they are its *imitatio*."[20] Both the society of the Gerasenes and the society of the demons have a structural unity, but it is a "unity in the process of disintegration" in the presence of Jesus. So the mob, the "crowd" of demons goes hurtling into the sea while the victim is left standing. It is the "crowd mentality" that leads the pigs to destroy themselves, the "irresistible tendency to mimeticism." And Girard concludes, "These pigs are truly possessed in that they are mimeticized up to their ears."[21]

[16] Ibid. 170. He is referring to Jean Starobinski, "The Gerasene Demoniac," in Roland Barthes et al., eds., *Structural Analysis and Biblical Exegesis* (Pittsburgh: Pickwick, 1974) 57–84. A shortened version appears in Jean Starobinski, "An Essay in Literary Analysis—Mark 5:1-20," *Ecumenical Review* 23 (1971) 377–97.

[17] Girard, *The Scapegoat*, 171.

[18] Ibid. 176.

[19] Ibid. 179.

[20] Ibid. 181.

[21] Ibid. 183.

Girard's mimetic theory seems to work well in understanding the Gerasene's story. He is the scapegoat who acts out the violence of his people, yet Jesus delivers him from this pathological relationship and sends the mob over the cliff instead of the victim.

3. "Winking" and "Bobbing" in Mimesis of Girard

Two New Testament scholars who have used Girard in their interpretation of the Gerasene are Walter Wink and Robert Hamerton-Kelly. We begin with Wink, who has already been mentioned in this chapter and the previous one. In the same year that the English translation of *The Scapegoat* appeared, 1986, the second volume of Walter Wink's trilogy on the Powers in the New Testament was published. It is entitled *Unmasking the Powers: The Invisible Forces that Determine Human Existence*. It discussed Satan, demons, angels, gods, and the "elements of the universe." The discussion of the Gerasene appeared in Chapter 2 on demons, which followed Chapter 1 on Satan.[22] In this chapter Wink distinguishes between personal and collective possession, and within the personal, between outer and inner personal possession. The Gerasene is an example of outer personal possession.

Although Wink says in the preface that Carl Jung and Elizabeth Boyden Howes (the director of the Jungian-oriented Guild for Psychological Studies) "have had a particularly profound impact on the themes developed here," it seems that his reading of the Gerasene story is more informed by Girard than Jung. He also uses some anthropological studies. Nevertheless, it is Girard's thought that forms the psychological and sociological backbone of his reading. Before turning to Girard, Wink sets the social location of the story. Gerasa, he notes, had been sacked by both Romans and Jews during the first Jewish revolt against Rome (66–70 C.E.). At the beginning of the revolt Jewish rebels sacked it, and just before besieging Jerusalem the Romans sacked and burned it and then quartered a legion there. In order to explore the demoniac's relationship to his social context, Wink turns to Girard's concept of "cyclical pathology" between the Gerasenes and their demons, in which the demoniac becomes the townspeople's scapegoat. "The townspeople need him to act out their own violence. He bears their collective madness personally, freeing them from their symptoms."[23]

Wink goes on to specify exactly what is being laid on the scapegoat. "Has this man not taken on himself the actual situation of the people? He

---

[22] Walter Wink, *Unmasking the Powers: The Invisible Forces that Determine Human Existence*. The Powers, vol. 2 (Philadelphia: Fortress, 1986) 43–50.

[23] Ibid. 46.

does what they would like to do: tear apart the chains and shatter the fetters of Roman authority. . . . But he had also internalized their captivity and the utter futility of resistance: he gashes himself with stones."[24]

Wink notes "the most curious aspect of our account: the substitutionary death of the pigs. *They* become the 'scapepigs' in place of the man, who is healed. Jesus thus breaks the vicious cycle of mimetic persecution."[25] Wink quotes Girard about the reversal of the crowd and the victim in this passage and about the demons as the image of the Gerasenes. Wink then adds, "The demons are the spirituality of the people," which continues the thesis that runs throughout his trilogy, that the Powers in the New Testament are the spirituality of the people.[26]

Wink concludes his reading of this story by saying that the demoniac was his society's deviant. He then asks: What do deviants tell us about their societies? He points to the navigator of the plane that dropped the atomic bomb on Hiroshima, who in the early 1960s was arrested for a series of petty crimes and committed to a mental institution. He also points to an adolescent who believes he is a Vietnam veteran who was killed in the war and is living a second life. Both these people are living out the violence for which society refuses to take responsibility. Wink concludes: "Outer personal possession thus reveals itself to be merely the personal pole of a collective malady afflicting an entire society."[27]

With Walter, we've "winked" at the Gerasene. Now let us "bob" with him with Hamerton-Kelly. In the early to mid 1990s Robert Hamerton-Kelly produced two books that were Girardian readings of New Testament texts, *Sacred Violence: Paul's Hermeneutic of the Cross* in 1992, and then just two years later *The Gospel and the Sacred: Poetics of Violence in Mark*.[28] Girard himself writes the Foreword for the book. (They were colleagues at Stanford at the time.) In his introduction Hamerton-Kelly gives a brief account of Girard's theory because he intends to take it as a guide to interpretation. Here he introduces the phrase "generative mimetic scapegoating mechanism" (GMSM). He writes, "It is generative because it generates the differences, it is mimetic because mimetic desire (not sexuality) drives it, it is scapegoating because it achieves its purpose by striking the

---

[24] Ibid.

[25] Ibid. 47.

[26] Ibid. 48. On p. 4 Wink states his thesis for all three volumes: "that the New Testament's 'principalities and powers' is a generic category referring to the determining forces of physical, psychic, and social existence."

[27] Ibid. 50

[28] Robert G. Hamerton-Kelly, *The Gospel and the Sacred: Poetics of Violence in Mark* (Minneapolis: Fortress, 1994).

surrogate victim, and it is a mechanism because it operates like a machine, systematically rather than deliberately."[29]

Hamerton-Kelly echoes Girard in speaking of the "double transference" of the mob's mimetic rivalry and its need for the victim to bring peace. When the victim is transformed into a god, the result is the primitive Sacred, with its prohibition, ritual, and myth. "The Gospel and the Sacred" of the book's title might be called The Gospel vs. the Sacred, for the Gospel serves to expose the lie of the GMSM. While the myth of the Sacred justifies the murderers, the Gospel vindicates the victim, arising from compassion for the victim. Like Girard, then, Hamerton-Kelly says that the Gospel is the opposite of myth.

Hamerton-Kelly's treatment of the Gerasene demoniac is surprisingly short, just over a page. Indeed, he refers to it as the "Gadarene" demoniac, though he nowhere discusses why he chooses this textual variant over "Gerasene." His discussion of the "Gadarene demoniac" appears in Chapter 4, entitled, "The Poetics of Faith: The Group and the Individual (4:1–10:52)." The first section in that chapter is called "Faith as the Dialectic of the Group and the Individual (4:1–6:56)." Hamerton-Kelly describes the demoniac as a "classic scapegoat figure." He carries his persecutors inside him in the "classic mode of the victim who internalizes his tormentors."[30] He mimes the persecution the townspeople would give him. The demonic legion is the lynch mob.

Like Girard, Hamerton-Kelly sees the herd of pigs rushing over the cliff as a mob in pursuit of its victim. Their drowning marks the end of the violence, for it is the mob that goes over the cliff rather than the victim. So Jesus threatens the Sacred of the Gadarenes, and they ask him to leave. They, therefore, understand Jesus better than the disciples, who have become, as shown in the calming of the sea, the "excluded insiders." As he leaves, Jesus sends the victim back to his own people. "[F]rom now on they have in their midst a constant reminder of an alternative to the order of violence in the restored and reintegrated victim whom Jesus rescued from the mob in himself and the mob in the city of Gadara."[31]

Girard, along with Wink and Hamerton-Kelly, brings into full relief the Gerasene as scapegoat upon whom the townspeople have projected their violence about Roman oppression. It helps us to see other scapegoats in the New Testament and in our world today.

---

[29] Ibid. 6–7.
[30] Ibid. 93.
[31] Ibid. 94.

Frantz Fanon

Girard is the only living theorist in my book, and Fanon is the only non-European. (Regrettably, I discuss no woman psychologist here.)[32] Fanon is considered one of the core thinkers of the twentieth century, though I had never heard of him until I came to Howard. (That shows how parochial my education had been!) I'm not even sure how I first came into contact with his work. Nevertheless, when I did finally get my hands on his classic little book *The Wretched of the Earth*, I was overwhelmed with his passion and insight. Furthermore, I have taken it as part of my mission to let the dominant culture know about the rich intellectual and cultural contributions of those of African descent. So let me help fulfill that mission by "introducing to some and presenting to others" the Afro-Caribbean psychiatrist Frantz Fanon.

1. Fanon's Story of Colonialism

Because Fanon's social context so explicitly informs his theories, we will spend a bit more time with his personal biography than we did with our other three theorists. Born in the Caribbean island of Martinique in 1925, he settled in France after fighting in World War II and received medical and psychiatric training. He considered himself French, but he was shocked to encounter French racism. So at the age of twenty-seven he wrote *Black Skin, White Masks*,[33] based on his experiences in France, Africa, and the Caribbean. He maintains that a racist culture makes it impossible for a black man to be psychologically healthy, for it alienates him from himself through "harmful psychological constructs." Even speaking French is self-alienating because it passes on the collective consciousness of the French that equates blackness with evil and sin. Blacks, then, are forced to wear white masks, thinking they can fully participate in an egalitarian society that accepts people regardless of skin color. As Deepika Bahri writes, "Cultural values are internalized, or 'epidermalized' into consciousness, creating a fundamental disjuncture between the black man's consciousness and his body. Under these conditions the black man is necessarily alienated from himself."[34]

---

[32] But see the discussion of psychoanalytic literary critics Julia Kristeva and Luce Irigaray in The Bible and Culture Collective, *The Postmodern Bible* (New Haven: Yale University Press, 1995) 212–22.

[33] Frantz Fanon, *Black Skin, White Masks,* trans. Charles Lam Markmann (New York: Grove Press, 1967). There is also a 1996 British film on Fanon with the same title, "Frantz Fanon: Black Skin, White Masks."

[34] Deepika Bahri, "Frantz Fanon" (18 May 2000), n. p. Postcolonial Studies at Emory Pages, 31 January 2004. Available: http://www.emory.edu/ENGLISH/Bahri/Fanon.html.

Though Fanon had been trained as a psychoanalyst, he saw the limitations of Freud in the colonial situation. Fanon writes about trying to understand a dream of someone in Madagascar:

> [T]he discoveries of Freud are of no use to us here. What must be done is to restore this dream *to its proper time*, and this time is the period during which eighty thousand natives were killed—that it to say, one of every fifty persons in the population; and *to its proper place*, and this place is an island of four million people, at the center of which no real relationship can be established, where dissension breaks out in every direction, where the only masters are lies and demagogy.[35]

Fanon later writes, "One should investigate the extent to which the conclusions of Freud or Adler can be applied to the effort to understand the man of color's view of the world."[36] He contends that the Oedipus complex is "far from coming into being among Negroes."[37] He further states that when the Negro comes into contact with the white world, his ego collapses because he finds his self-esteem in pleasing The Other, who is for him the white man.

In 1953 Fanon became head of the psychiatric department at a hospital in Algeria, which at that time was a colony of France. While he was there, the war for Algerian independence broke out, and Fanon was appalled at the torture to which his patients gave witness. He resigned his post in 1956 in order to work for the Algerian independence movement, first in Tunisia and then in Ghana. While in Ghana, he developed leukemia. He wrote his final and most fiery work, *The Wretched of the Earth,* in ten months. It was published with a Foreword by Jean Paul Sartre in 1961, the year of Fanon's death.

In his "Wretched" book, Fanon writes about the "Manicheism" of colonialism, in which the colonized world is sliced in two: between the colonizers, who have everything, and the colonized, who have nothing. This "Manicheism" is maintained through violence, both the physical violence of armaments and the psychological and emotional violence of identifying the colonized as absolute evil. The colonized work inside this framework. They either accept it, that is, they accept their identification as absolute evil, or they flip the framework, and they identify the colonizers as absolute evil.[38]

[35] Fanon, *Black Skin,* 104. Italics in original.
[36] Ibid. 141.
[37] Ibid. 152.
[38] Frantz Fanon, *The Wretched of the Earth,* trans. Constance Farrington (New York: Grove Press, 1963) 37–54. Manicheism was a third- to fifth-century religious movement that posited a radical dualism between good and evil and between body and spirit.

Fanon continues that the colonized accommodate their oppression by mystifying it. Fate or god or the devil or demons are responsible for their plight. He writes: "A belief in fatality removes all blame from the oppressor; the cause of misfortunes and of poverty is attributed to God: He is Fate. In this way the individual accepts the disintegration ordained by God, bows down before the settler and his lot, and by a kind of interior restabilization acquires a stony calm."[39]

Fanon goes on to say, "The supernatural, magical powers reveal themselves as essentially personal; the settler's powers are infinitely shrunken, stamped with their alien origin. We no longer really need to fight against them since what counts is the frightening enemy created by myths. We perceive that all is settled by a permanent confrontation on the phantasmic [i.e., spirit] plane."[40] The colonizers then are let off the hook. They are not at fault for these wrongs. Rather, it is the fault of these gods or the devil or demons. This absolving of wrongdoing is beneficial because often when the colonized take up arms it results in widespread violence and further repression by the colonizers. Yet it is only partially beneficial because it prevents the colonized from coming to consciousness about their political situation.

Fanon maintains that a study of the colonial world must include a study of dance and possession. He writes, "The native's relaxation takes precisely the form of a muscular orgy in which the most acute aggressivity and the most impelling violence are canalized, transformed, and conjured away."[41] The purpose of these ritual dances is to "allow the accumulated libido, the hampered aggressivity to dissolve as in a volcanic eruption."[42] Fanon speaks of organized séances of possession and exorcism. He writes:

> This disintegrating of personality, this splitting and dissolution, all this fulfills a primordial function in the organism of the colonized world. When they set out, the men and women were impatient, stamping their feet in a state of nervous excitement; when they return, peace has been restored to the village; it is once more calm and unmoved.[43]

In the last chapter of the book Fanon has a long list in which he catalogs the mental illnesses that arose during French colonialism and the

---

[39] Ibid. 54–55.
[40] Ibid. 56.
[41] Ibid. 57.
[42] Ibid.
[43] Ibid.

Algerian revolution, including psychoses, neuroses, depression, and delir-
ium, often leading to suicidal or homicidal tendencies.[44] He relates one particular interesting story. A twenty-two-year-old felt so guilty for not
participating in revolutionary activity that he became physically emaciated
and mentally deranged. He heard voices that accused him of cowardice.
Once he tried to find relief from these voices through getting French soldiers to kill him. He said, "All I wanted to do was to die." Fanon notes that
cases like this were quite common in Algeria.[45]

Fanon spotlights the psychological disintegration associated with the
colonial context. This "Manichean" world results in demon possession and
exorcism and in mental illness.

2. Hollenbach and Horsley "Fanon" the Flame

Among New Testament scholars, two "Fanon fans" are Paul Hollenbach and Richard Horsley, for *The Wretched of the Earth* has been very influential in their attempts to understand the Gerasene story. (Both of these
scholars have made wide use of the social sciences in their biblical inter-
pretations in general.) First we will look at Hollenbach, and then turn to
Horsley.

Hollenbach discusses the Gerasene in an oft-cited article entitled,
"Jesus, Demoniacs, and Public Authorities: A Socio-Historical Study."[46] He
maintains that like Fanon's Algeria, Jesus' Palestine was also experiencing
oppressive colonialism and that such an environment, characterized by
domination and revolution, nourished mental illness. He writes, "Mental illness can be seen as a socially acceptable form of oblique protest against, or
escape from, oppressions."[47] He follows Fanon when, in his discussion of
"psychosomatic pathology," Fanon says that "an organism . . . resolves the
conflict by unsatisfactory, but on the whole economical means. The organism in fact chooses the lesser evil in order to avoid catastrophe."[48]

Hollenbach notes that the Gerasene demoniac is quite similar to the
guilt-ridden young man discussed by Fanon. He further suggests, follow-

---

[44] Ibid. 249–310.

[45] Ibid. 272–75.

[46] Paul W. Hollenbach, "Jesus, Demoniacs, and Public Authorities: A Socio-Historical
Study," *Journal of the American Academy of Religion* 99 (1981) 567–88. See also his "Help
for Interpreting Jesus' Exorcisms," *Society of Biblical Literature Seminar Papers* 32 (Atlanta: Scholars, 1993) 119–28.

[47] Hollenbach, "Jesus, Demoniacs, and Public Authorities," 575.

[48] Ibid., quoting Fanon, *The Wretched of the Earth*, 290.

ing Fanon, that the Gerasene's possession is both disease and cure. The Gerasene was torn between his hatred for the Romans and his need to repress that hatred, and thus went mad.

> But his very madness permitted him to do in a socially acceptable manner what he could not do as sane, namely express his total hostility to the Romans; he did this by identifying the Roman legions with demons. His possession was thus at once both the result of oppression and an expression of his resistance to it. He retreated to an inner world where he could symbolically resist Roman domination.[49]

Jesus, however, disrupted the "social stability" of the Gerasenes' situation by offering "social healing" not just to the one possessed, but also to the Gerasenes.[50] They, however, rejected it and asked Jesus to take his social healing elsewhere.

Richard Horsley, in his recent book entitled *Hearing the Whole Story: The Politics of Plot in Mark's Gospel,* also uses Fanon in understanding this passage.[51] He finds particularly helpful Fanon's idea of the colonial world as a "Manichean world." Horsley maintains that the people of Jesus' day developed a Manicheism that explained why pagans were ruling over them in the land God had given them. They said that superhuman forces, such as Satan, were currently in charge of history, but that God, who was ultimately in charge of history, would soon defeat Satan and restore the land to God's control.

Horsley also finds helpful Fanon's discussion of the function of demon possession and exorcism in the colonial context. He writes concerning ancient Palestine, "Belief in demons helped enable the people to persist in the Israelite faith and way of life. By blaming superhuman evil forces for their sufferings Galileans and Judeans could avoid blaming themselves as well as God."[52] He continues,

> Demon possession . . . of the manically violent man among the Gerasenes can be understood as a combination of the effect of Roman imperial violence, a displaced protest against it, and a self-protection against a suicidal counterattack against the Romans. . . . The demoniac

---

[49] Ibid. 581.

[50] Ibid. 584.

[51] Richard A. Horsley, *Hearing the Whole Story: The Politics of Plot in Mark's Gospel* (Louisville: Westminster John Knox, 2001) 141–48.

[52] Ibid. 144–45.

became the repository of the community's resentment of the violent effects of Roman domination.[53]

Horsley says that attributing oppression to superhuman forces was both "an enabling revelation and a diversionary mystification."[54] It enabled the people to go on living their traditional way of life, but it also blinded them to the political and economic realities of Roman rule.

Jesus, however, in the exorcism of the Gerasene pulls back the veil of mystification. By eliciting the demoniac's name as Legion he suggests that the struggle is really against Roman rule. This struggle, furthermore, will end in the people's liberation from Legion, as shown in the pigs drowning in the sea. (Horsley notes how their drowning in the sea echoes the Exodus story of the Egyptians drowning in the sea in Exod 15:1-10.)

> The casting out and naming of "Legion" is a demystification of (the belief in) demons and demon possession. It is now evident to Jesus' followers and to the hearers of Mark's story that the struggle is really against the rulers, ultimately the Romans. And the story now focuses accordingly on Jesus' confrontation of the Roman client rulers of Israel and eventually with the Romans themselves in his trial and crucifixion.[55]

Fanon demonstrates that demons, demon possession, and exorcism serve as social control in the colonial context, as they mystify the oppressive powers. Hollenbach and Horsley, building on Fanon, show that Jesus brought social healing rather than social stability, that he demystified the demons, showing that the real culprit was Rome.

Conclusion

René Girard and Frantz Fanon are not household names in either psychology or biblical studies, but perhaps they should be. They focus our attention on the social-psychological situation of the Gerasene so that we are not mired in his (or our!) individual psychology. We see that Legion is not only the Gerasene demoniac but also the Gerasenes' demoniac, for he serves as scapegoat for his people. We also see that Legion bears the ravages of colonialism, and in his exorcism the demons are demystified, so that we realize that the real battle is against the imperial power Rome.

[53] Ibid. 145.
[54] Ibid.
[55] Ibid. 147.

So what have we been doing here? What's in our hands? In one hand we've got theory, and in the other we've got a story. Then we've brought them together. What is in our hands now? Do the theory and the story fit together? Do they fit, or do they fight? Where are the connections? Where is the slippage? What do you think?

Think now about this question: How can we put it all together? In this part we've done Freud, Jung, Girard, and Fanon, not to mention the previous part when we've done Chatman. But we're not done. In the next section we try to bring all these perspectives together as we read the story with (New)heart and soul. Right on! Read on!

CHAPTER SIX

Reading Legion's Story with (New)Heart and Soul[1]

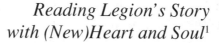

So, how can we put it all together? Is there a way to bring together narrative and psychological biblical criticism, integrate Chatman, Freud, Jung, Girard, and Fanon? Probably not, but I'm going give it the old college try! I offer here my own "soul reading" of the story. It has been influenced by all the theorists we have discussed. I sometimes call it a playful and poetic reading. My soul reading is, like the other readings I've discussed, an interpretation of the text. It is not *the* interpretation any more than the others are. Again, we're looking for a "fit." (I hope you won't throw a fit!) Although we biblical critics act as though it's not true, interpretation is very much experimental; it is simply trying out various constructions of a text. In many ways it's like shopping for shoes: you try on a pair and walk around for a while; if they feel good, you buy them and wear them.

So, walk a mile in my shoes! I hope they don't hurt your feet! Here's what I'm going to do in this chapter: I will first describe what a soul reading is, and then I will demonstrate it on the Gerasene story.

Reading with Soul

What does it mean to read a story "soulfully"? I have discussed my "soul reading" at length in previous publications, so I will merely summa-

[1] An earlier version of this chapter was published as "Legion: A Violent Soul in a Violent Society (Mark 5:1-20)," in J. Harold Ellens, ed., *The Destructive Power of Religion: Violence in Judaism, Christianity, and Islam* (Westport, CT: Praeger, 2004) 2:199–217. I am grateful to the editor and to Praeger for permission to publish here.

rize here.[2] My soul reading is psychological, literary, and cultural, for it brings together analytical and archetypal psychology, African-American cultural experience, and reader-response criticism.

1. Analytical and Archetypal Psychology

The psychological aspect comes from analytical and archetypal psychology, which attempts to bring "soul" back into psychology. We discussed the analytical psychology of Carl Jung in Chapter 4. Jung writes often of "soul."[3] He says, "The reality of the soul is the reality upon which I work."[4] He considers psychotherapy "the treatment of the soul," for "the soul is the birthplace of all action and everything that happens by the will of [hu]man[ity]."[5] He points to the Bible as a "soul-book," for "the statements made in the Holy Scriptures are also utterances of the soul . . . [T]hey always go over our heads because they point to realities that transcend consciousness."[6]

James Hillman, who stands to Jung as Lacan stands to Freud, takes Jung's emphasis on soul and twists it in his own brand of psychology, which he calls "archetypal psychology." He defines soul as "a perspective rather than a substance, a viewpoint rather than a thing itself."[7] Hillman continues that the fantasy images are the primary data of the soul and the privileged mode of access to knowledge of the soul. He contends that in order to get to the soul of the image (or the image of soul) one must "love the image," that is, stick with it and twist it by doing wordplays, for the words are "soul mines."[8] He further maintains that one deepens the image

---

[2] See Michael Willett Newheart, *Word and Soul: A Psychological, Literary, and Cultural Reading of the Fourth Gospel*, Michael Glazier Books (Collegeville: Liturgical Press, 2001) xiv–xxi. The book's introduction, in which these pages are found, can be read online at http://www. litpress.org/Store/excerpt.cfm?ID=2173. See also my "Soul 2 Soul: A Post-Modern Exegete in Search of (New Testament) Soul," *Journal of Religious Thought* 55.2–56.1 (2000) 1–17.

[3] In the index to his collected works, the listings for "soul(s)," "soul(s) in alchemy," "soul and spirit," and "soul-images" take up over three pages. Cf. the General Index to *The Collected Works of C. G. Jung* (hereafter *CW*) (Princeton: Princeton University Press, 1979), 20:624–27. (I refer to the volume and page number of the English translation of *CW*.)

[4] Quoted in Hans Schaer, *Religion and the Cure of Souls in Jung's Psychology*, trans. R.F.C. Hull. Bollingen Series 21 (New York: Pantheon, 1950) 21.

[5] C. G. Jung, "Psychotherapy Today," *The Practice of Psychotherapy: Essays on the Psychology of the Transference and Other Subjects*, 2nd ed., *CW* 16:94.

[6] C. G. Jung, "Answer to Job," *Psychology and Religion: West and East*, 2nd ed., *CW* 11:362. The term "soul-book" is mine, not Jung's.

[7] James Hillman, *Re-Visioning Psychology* (New York: Harper & Row, 1975) x.

[8] James Hillman, "An Inquiry into Image," *Spring* 39 (1977) 81–82.

by making analogies, or likenesses, for the images. What is this image like? Analogies, according to Hillman, "keep the image there, alive and well, returning to it each time for a fresh sense of it."[9]

Like Jung and Hillman, I am searching for soul, for my soul, for the biblical soul. Analytical and archetypal psychology encourage me to find soul in the images, so I focus on the biblical images. And with what Hillman calls "a poetic basis of mind," I open up these images (and my own soul) by twisting them and doing wordplays with them. Furthermore, I also open up the images by finding contemporary analogies, or likenesses, for them.

2. African-American Cultural Experience

My soul reading is shaped not only by analytical and archetypal psychology but also by the cultural experience of persons of African descent. African-American experience is often referred to as "soul," as African Americans have given us "soul music" and "soul food," and they refer to one another as "soul brother" and "soul sister." In the United States, then, persons of African descent have been the carriers of soul. African-American soul, however, has been described variously. I have found the most satisfactory definition in *Roots of Soul: The Psychology of Black Expressiveness* by Alfred Pasteur and Ivory Toldson. They identify soul with black expressiveness, which is based in rhythm. They write, "Rhythm is the thread that runs through the fabric of black culture; it is therefore at the base of black expressive behavior."[10] As poet Guy Tirolier says: "(I want to proclaim out loud // that life is only rhythm // and rhythm within a rhythm)."[11] Furthermore, Pasteur and Toldson identify five elements of soul, or black expressiveness: depth of feeling, naturalistic attitudes, stylistic renderings, poetic and prosaic vernacular, and expressive movement.[12] In their chapter on depth of feeling, the authors say that soul is "the ability to feel and express feelings creatively, or through forms touched with artistic sensibilities."[13]

One such form of "artistic sensibility" is poetry, in which African Americans have contributed significantly to world literature. Poetry has

---

[9] Ibid. 86–87. Hillman develops his approach to image further in "Further Notes on Images," *Spring* 40 (1978) 152–82, and "Image-Sense," *Spring* 41 (1979) 130–43.

[10] Alfred B. Pasteur and Ivory L. Toldson, *Roots of Soul: The Psychology of Black Expressiveness* (Garden City, NY: Doubleday, 1982) 4.

[11] E. A. Hurley, "Guy Tirolier: In search of an attitude," *Black Images* 3/1 (1974) 61, quoted in Pasteur and Toldson, *Roots of Soul*, 59.

[12] Ibid. 10.

[13] Ibid. 103.

often been called the voice of the soul, so African-American poetry might be considered the "soul of soul." African-American poetry shapes my soul hermeneutic in two ways: my poetic readings of the biblical images reflect the rhythms of this poetry, and I find the likenesses to these images in this body of literature.

3. Reader-Response Criticism

The final element of my soul reading is reader-response criticism, which is a "kissing cousin" (sometimes "*distant* cousin") of narrative criticism. Some reader-response critics make much of the "implied reader," to use Chatman's terminology.[14] Other reader-response critics, however, focus on what Chatman calls the "real reader." This reader has a personal story that affects the reading of the text and, using autobiography, these reader-response critics tell their stories to illuminate the reading of the text. This reader also has a certain "social location," which includes race, gender, class, sexual orientation, and religious affiliation. In my soul reading I attempt to do justice to the reader's "soul-state," which encompasses a reader's psychological and social dynamics. For example, I am a middle-class, European-American, heterosexual, Christian (Quaker, specifically) intellectual male teaching in a predominantly African-American institution. Also, I take into consideration various emotional issues that I'm wrestling with. As I note in the Introduction, I struggle with generalized anxiety disorder and depression.[15]

The "soul reading," then, is the reading of the soul of the text *and* the soul of the reader, that is, my own soul. A synonym for "soul" might be "depths." "Deep calls to deep," the Psalmist says (42:7). I explore the depths of a text and my own depths, attempting to bring the two into dialogue.

There you have my soul reading, which consists of analytical and archetypal psychology, African-American cultural experience, and reader-response criticism. I now turn my attention to a soul reading of Mark 5:1-20. I will first present a poetic translation of the story. Next I poetically play with its images. Then I find likenesses to these images by exploring images of violence in contemporary African-American poetry. Finally, I briefly discuss the likenesses to the images in my own soul.

Before we proceed, though, I must warn you that my "soul reading" is not representative of the current state of biblical studies. Although some parts of it have resonances in the work of other scholars (e.g., the wordplay

---

[14] See above, Chapter 1, 11–12.
[15] See above, Introduction, xxi.

and the autobiography), it really is unique. So don't get the impression that
biblical studies in general is this much fun!—though I think it can be, as
people allow themselves to take the text more seriously, and therefore play
with it.

So(ul) let us go!

A "Soulful," Poetic Translation of the Story

Following is the translation of the story that appeared in the introduction.[16] I have made two changes. First, I have arranged the story on the
page in a poetic fashion, both to highlight its structure and to emphasize
(or play with) certain words or phrases. Second, I have italicized some of
the words that appear repeatedly either in this story or in the Gospel of
Mark.

I suggest that you read it aloud, as you might do with the following
section too. But don't just *read* it aloud; shout it, whisper it, sing it, sign it,
dance it, do with it whatever you feel is right, except, of course, discard it!
So, go for it!

And they came

          to   the other side of the *sea,*

          to   the region   of the Gerasenes.

And when Jesus got out of the *boat,*

suddenly there met him

              out of the *tombs*

a man

        with an   *unclean spirit,*

who was living   among   the *tombs,*

and no one   could   restrain him any longer,

not even with   a *chain,*

for he'd been bound with *fetters* and *chains*   many times,

but he'd   torn   apart the *chains*

and   s m a s h e d   the *fetters,*

and no one   was *strong* enough to tame him.

And every night

     and day

    in the *tombs*

---

[16] See above, xix–xx.

and on the *mountains*
he was   *screaming*
and   gashing himself   with stones.

And when he *saw* Jesus   from a distance,
he ran
and fell down in front of him,
and he *screams* with a *great* voice and says,
    "WHAT'VE YOU GOT AGAINST ME,
    JESUS SON OF THE HIGHEST *GOD?*
    I SWEAR TO YOU BY *GOD,*
    DON'T TORTURE ME!"
For Jesus was about to say to him,
    "Come out   of the man,
    you *unclean spirit!*"
And Jesus asked him,
    "What's your *name?*"
He said to him,
    "*Legion*   's my *name,*
    for   we're many."
And he *begged* Jesus
wildly
not to send them   out of the region.
Now on   the *mountainside*
was a *great herd*   of *pigs*   *grazing.*
And the *spirits begged* him,
    "Send us   into   the *pigs,*
    so we can enter them."
And he let them.
And the *unclean spirits* exited the man
and entered the *pigs.*
And the *herd,*
      about two thousand strong,
rushed down a steep bank
    into the *sea,*
and they were drowned
    in the *sea.*

And the ones *grazing* the *pigs*   ran off

and told   what had happened
in   the city
and the country,
and people   *came* to *see.*
And they   *come* to   Jesus
and they *see* the *demonized* man,
                         the man who had had the *legion,*
seated, dressed and sane,
and they were *afraid.*

And those who had *seen* what had happened
                                      to the *demonized* one
also recounted to them   about the *pigs*
And they began *begging* Jesus to   get out   of their country.

And as he got   into the *boat,*
the *ex-demonized* one   begged Jesus to be with him,
but Jesus didn't let him;
rather, he says to him,
    "Go home   to your own people,
      and tell   them   *what the Lord has done for you*
                         and how he's had compassion on you."
And the man left
and began preaching
              in the Ten Cities
                         what Jesus had done for him.
And everyone was amazed.

Playing with the Images of the Story

Following is a playful, poetic commentary on the passage. Yes, playful and poetic . . . and possessed! A story about a man possessed by a legion of unclean spirits and a man possessed by the Holy Spirit calls for a possessed commentary! So you will encounter misspellings, poor syntax, ungrammatical expressions, inconsistent capitalization and punctuation . . . and plenty of puns, puns, puns. (You might think that you're being *pun*-ished!)[17] And what is this playful, poetic, possessed commentary possessed by? An unclean spirit or the Holy Spirit? Good question. We'll see.

---

[17] To hearken back to our discussion of Freud in Chapter 4, I am attempting to adhere to the "pleasure principle" instead of the "reality principle." I noted above in this chapter that

Again, I think it would be helpful if you read the following section aloud. Also, feel free to move about as you read.

So our story begins, though Mark has begun a long time ago: "The beginning of the good news of Jesus Christ, Son of God" (Mark 1:1). So this is the "middle" of the good news of Jesus Christ, Son of God. Because we're beginning in the middle, we have a lot of catching up to do. Mark begins his Gerasene story: "And they came to the other side of the sea." They? Who "they"? Hoo dey? Jesus and the disciples. Jee-zus and de ddddisciples. Jesus? Yes, Jesus, that messianic sonagod (1:1), baptized-holyspirit-into-him (1:9-10), disciple calling (1:16-20; 2:13-14), unclean-spiritanddemon-outcasting (1:21-28, 34, 39, etc.), diseased-healing (1:34, 40-45, etc.), scribesandPharisees-roiling (2:1-12, 15-17, etc.), parable-speaking (4:1-34), windandsea-peace-be-stilling (4:35-41) Jesus. Yes, him.

But not just Jesus (though Jesus is certainly just), also his disciples. Duh ddddisciples. And it seems that they are always saying, "Duh!" After the windsea calming, they say, "Duh! Hoo den is dis dat—who then is this—that even wind&sea obey him?" (4:41) You knuckleheads! Don't you listen to the narrator (1:1), to the voice from heaven (1:10), to the unclean spirits (3:11) dat say dat dis iz de sonagod, that say that this is the Son of God!? Man, that Gentile Roman centurion knows more than you (15:39). He knows, he nose, has the nose for news, the good news, that Jesus was sonagod. But da disciples don't get it, not in this sea crossing or any of the others (hearts hardened at water-walking, 6:47-52; misunderstanding Jesus' yeasty-words, 8:14-21).

Things don't get any better for them. Sure, they cross the sea . . . but they don't see the cross. Each time Jesus passion-predicts, disciples misunderstand (8:31-33; 9:30-32; 10:32-40). In this passionate section blind men seeing (8:22-26; 10:45-52) frames seeing folks (i.e., dddisciples) blinded What's wrong with them? They have been given the secret of the God's reign (4:11); they've been called to be with Jesus and preach and cast out demons (3:13-19a), which they do (6:7-13); but they don't quite get it. Don't quite, so they quit. They forsake Jesus—in the garden, which is not paradise for them (14:50). Indeed, they disappear from the scene in this story: no mention of them after the first line. Where are they? Have they drowned in the sea?

So Jesus and his disciples go to the other side of the sea, that is, the other side of the Sea of Galilee (1:16). On this side, he's been fishing for

---

Hillman's relation to Jung was much like that of Lacan to Freud. Indeed, my "playing with the images" in this section is very similar to Lacan's method because he also uses wordplays, witticisms, and puns. See his *Écrits: A Selection*, trans. Alan Sheridan (New York: Norton, 1977).

folk who are Jews. Now he goes to the other side to fish for folk who are Gentiles. Gentle Gentiles? Not according to Jesus, who chauvinistically calls them "dogs" (7:27). So Jesus's fishing for dogs here on the other side.

Jesus and disciples go to other side of the sea, to the region of the Gerasenes (garish scene?). Gerasenes, where people of Gerasa live. But hey, get out your map: Gerasa's not within hollerin' distance a de sea a galilee. What? Thirty-some miles! Hmm. Mark has moved Gerasa next to the sea. Things are already gettin' eery. But stay tuned!

So Jesusanddisciples come to the sea's other side, to the Gerasene region. And Jesus gets outa de boat. (Do da da disciples stay in de boat?) So Jesus get outa de boat, de boat dats been his lectern as well as bunk (Mark 4:1, 38). When Jesus get outa d boat—wham! suddenly immediately straightway (I like dat ol' KingJamesVersionBible term.) things always happenin' in Mark immediately straightway wham! It's a fast-paced book (huff-puff) Jesus in a hurry for example chapter one comeup outa water Wham! heavenrip spiritcomedown voice Wham! Spirit throws him out into wilderness (1:10-12), Capernaumsynagogue teaching Wham! uncleanspirited man (1:21-23), leave synagogue Wham! enter SimonAndrewshouse (1:29-31), beggingkneeling skin-diseased man "Be clean" Wham! skin disease go bye-bye and he clean (1:40-42).

Now, Jesus outa d boat Wham! met by dis coming-outa-d-tombs-with-unclean-spirit-man. A man amen a man a hu-man who-man with (in?) an unclean (profane, not-profound) spirit—spirited uncleanness, outta-place spirit, unclensed breath, impure wind. Spirit, spit it out! Not first unclean Jesus seen. Began Galilee gig (his Jewish jaunt) by exorcizing (exercising? hit de deck & gimme five!) an unclean spirit, cleanly showing his new authoritative teaching (1:21-28). Now begins Gentile juggernaut by exorcizing unclean spirit. And dis spirit was quite unclean cuz it put dis guy in de tombs, an unclean place for Jewish sensibilities. Three times Mark associates him with the tombs (5:2, 3, 5). Not only is this man's spirit unclean, but he's also dead! And folks try to chain and fetter him. To keep him from going to the tombs? To keep him from leaving the tombs? Whatever their reasons, the unclean spirited (U.S.?) man rips de chains and smashes de fetters. Rip (like de heavens, 1:10?) and smash! But binding and freeing happens "manytimes." It seems that the people are chained and fettered to the U.S.man. Remember Girard and *The Scapegoat?* He talks about the "cyclical pathology" of the townspeople and the U.S.man and about the violent and ritualistic character of the people's actions toward him.[18] You may also remember that Walter Wink, building on Girard, says

[18] See above, Chapter 5, 74.

that the demons are the spirituality of the people.[19] So the man and the people are chained and fettered together! But while the people are bound, the U.S. man is free: he breaks his bonds. He is the satanically strong man who can't be bound (3:26-27). He is the wild animal, whom no one NO ONE can tame. (Down boy, down!) (Jesus will soon be with this diabolically wild beast, 1:13.)

This wildly strong, beasty boy would roam among the tombs and on the mountains (go tell it on the mountain!) SCREAMING, and no wonder he was doing that because he was also self-stone-cutting. (Simon's not the only Rocky in this story, 3:16.) Taking on de punishment de people wanna give him? Chaining and stoning. Girard: "an example of the reciprocal relationship of mimetic rivalry."[20] People with (unclean?) spirits in Mark often engage in self-mutilation: See case of boy with mute spirit who throws him into fire water to kill him (9:22). Maybe they are taking on society's violent condemnation of them by trying to destroy their spirits by destroying themselves. (Indeed, Jesus' spirit leads him to the cross!)

Once the U.S.man had had enough tomb dwelling, chain-smashing, night&day screaming, self-stoning, he sees distant Jesus shoring up and he runrunrunrunruns to him and kneels before him (like the U.S.s usually do, 3:11). He realizes that Jesus is a holy spirited man—H.S.man— much more powerful than U.S.man. This strong man knows that this one can bind him and plunder his house (3:27). So he screams even more terribly: "WHAT'VE YOU AGAINST ME, JESUS SON OF THE HIGHEST GOD? I SWEAR TO YOU BY GOD, DON'T TORTURE ME!" Much like the Capernaum U.S.man, who screamed too (though not terribly), "WHAT'VE YOU GOT TO DO WITH US, JESUS OF NAZARETH? DID YOU COME TO DESTROY US? I KNOW WHO YOU ARE: GOD'S HOLY ONE!" (1:24) U.S.men must have a set speech they learn in U.S. training when they meet H.S.men: first, they ask what the H.S.man has to do with me/us; then, they call the H.S.man by name and title (Capernaum U.S.man gives Jesus' hometown, which is also in the Galilee, and says that he's God's holy one, while the Gerasene calls Jesus sonofGod, like the seeing, kneeling, shouting U.S.s, 3:11, like the narrator, 1:1, God, 1:11, and like the executing centurion, 15:39; does the centurion have the spirit now? the disciples most certainly don't); then, they talk about destruction or torment. The Gerasene swears by God, Jesus' father, not to be tortured. If he doesn't want to be tortured, then why did he run to Jesus anyway? Jesus does tell the U.S. to exit,

---

[19] See above, Chapter 5, 77.
[20] See above, Chapter 5, 75.

but he doesn't silence the Gerasene as he did the Capernaum U.S.man and the usual U.S.s. (Ssshhh! It's a secret, a messianic secret.)[21]

Instead, he asks the Gerasene his name. Presumably, Jesus already knows his name, but the reader doesn't, so Jesus has him introduce himself. He says that his name's Legion, for "we're many." Legion, huh? Oh! Now that explains a lot. "Legion" is a military term for a division of Roman soldiers, numbering about six thousand. Yes, yes, things are starting to fall into place. This man, possessed by a legion of demons, is representative of his people, who themselves are possessed by a legion of Roman soldiers. He acts out what they are living. No wonder they want to chain him, just as they are chained. But he breaks free. Indeed, he's the freest man in the region, for he "acts out" rather than submits to imperial conquest. So he's liberated from, yet bound to, their projection. He becomes their scapegoat, and he does it so well that they don't even have to stone him (which they would like to do to the blasphemous Romans), for he stones himself! He internalizes their self-hatred.

So Legion, huh? Jesus' contemporaries have "mystified" Roman oppression through talk about demons, but Jesus pulls back the veil of mystification. (Remember Frantz Fanon and Richard Horsley's use of his thought.)[22] It's time to wake up from our demonic slumber and see who's really been giving us fits, who's the real strong man binding us! Time to withdraw those projections and become conscious!

Yes, his name is Legion We're Many. Manymanymany. (Miniminimini?) In twenty-first-century shrinkspeak, one might say that he has Multiple Personality Disorder. Rome's New World Order has brought him Disorder! So dis disordered demoniac then begs Jesus not to send the many outa de region a de Gerasenes. They're unclean spirits, and they wanna live in this uncleen place. The Roman legions don't wanna leave the territory they're occupying. They're grounded in that ground!

Mark then widens his narrative lens and shows the reader a herda pigs on the mountainside. It's a great herda pigs. Had ya hearda da herda pigs? The spirits see it too. They (not the spirited man but the spirit themselves) negotiate with Jesus concerning their being cast out. They urge him to send them into the pigs (oink oink). Pigs after all are unclean animals according to the Jews, and that would be a good place for unclean spirits, in uncleen animals. Also they're often used as symbols for Romans in literature of the day.[23] So Jesus grants the U.S. request. And the unclean spirits leave the

---

[21] See above, Chapter 2, 22.

[22] See above, Chapter 5, 81, 84.

[23] See Warren Carter, *Matthew and the Margins: A Sociopolitical and Religious Reading* (Maryknoll, NY: Orbis, 2000) 212–13.

man and enter the pigs (oink OINK oink OINK OINK). Then they rush off a cliff into the sea (OINKOINKOINKOINKOINKOINKOINK—KER-SPLASH!). And there are about two thousand of them. (Does that mean that there were two or three unclean spirits per pig?) They become the "scapepigs,"[24] and they, rather than the man, go off the cliff.[25] And dey're drowned in the sea (oink . . . oink . . . glub . . . glub . . . glub), drowned like the Egyptians, who drowned in the Red Sea.[26] I'm sure that the U.S. didn't plan on that! So the U.S. legion drowns in the sea, pointing toward what the folks of that region long for: the Roman legions drowning in the sea, thus initiating a new Exodus. The violent Roman oppressors will meet a violent end! By God![27]

The piggrazers hightail it outa there and tell what had happened and cityandcountryfolk come to see. They see not only Jesus but also de demonized dude, de former legionaire, seated, shirted and sane. Seated, shirted and sane oh my! Oh my, they say, cuz they were SCARED, like de ddddisciples n de boat (4:41). In Mark fear and faith don't go together. These folk are fearful, faithless ones. Perhaps they even asked, "Who then is this, that even a legion of demons obey him?" (see 4:41) And the witnesses of the pigpossessionanddrowning tell their story, and so they beg Jesus (people and spirits always begging Jesus to do something, 5:10, 12) to get out out out. Outa their region, the region of the Gerasenes. This is an unclean region; how dare you clean it up for us! Besides, we had a nice little sick relationship with this guy and the Roman demonic legions, and you messed it up. So get the hell, er, heaven, outa here!

Jesus is pretty compliant in this passage when conscious beings "beg" him to do something, so he leaves. He gets into the boat . . . but there's one more request. The ex-demonized one wants to be with Jesus, to be like one of the Twelve, who've been appointed (on the mountain!) to be with him and to be sent out to preach and to cast out demons (3:13-15). Now that would be pretty cool, wouldn't it? He had a legion a demons, Jesus cast them out, and then he could cast out demons from others. But Jesus doesn't agree to beggar's request this time. Perhaps he doesn't want this Gentile among his Jewish followers. They are fearful and faithless; they don't know that he's the Son of God, which this guy does. In many ways he, like other Markan minor characters (e.g., woman with a hemorrhage,

---

[24] This is Wink's term. See above, Chapter 5, 77.

[25] This is Girard's insight. See above, Chapter 5, 75.

[26] This is Horsley's insight. See above, Chapter 5, 84.

[27] If Mark was written during the first revolt against Rome (66–70), as is usually thought, then this image of legions being drowned in the sea would have been particularly relevant for the first readers of the gospel.

5:25-34; Bartimaeus, 10:46-52), replaces the disciples. Jesus tells him to go back home (Jesus doesn't want to send him out of the region) and tell folks (like the pigfarmers have dun) what the master, the Lord, YHWH God, the highest God, the Jewish God, has done for him, and how he's "mercied" him, had compassion on him, suffered with him (literal meaning of the English word "com-passion") and healed him of his sufferings. So it is the compassion of God, the divine desire, the Lord's longing, flowing through Jesus that has de-demonized this man (just as it will sight blind Bartimaeus, 10:47-48). No need now to keep it a secret (unlike the ex-skin-diseased man, 1:44).

So the man (and he is the Man now . . . but what's his name?) goes away. Is he disappointed? sad? excited? Dunno. Nevertheless, he begins preaching, proclaiming the gospel (John, Jesus, and apostle-like, 1:4, 14; 3:14) in the Ten Cities of de Decapolis, of which Gerasa is one. (Through his efforts and that of others, the gospel is preached to all the Gentiles, 13:10). This man's gospel is about what the masterlord Jesus has done for him. (Is he obedient to his commission or not?) And all de Decapolitans who heard him are amazed (like Pilate is amazed later on, 15:5; will they too crucify Jesus?). They're amazed into silence. What do they say? What do they do?

And what happens to de Man? Mark leaves him in de Decapolis. Does he become an itinerant? Does he go back to the Gerasene region? Does he form, wherever he is, a community of Jesus-followers that are fulla clean spirits, the Holy Spirit? I like to think that he begins living by Jesus' teachings and he becomes again a man possessed, this time not by a violent legion of demons but by a spirit of peace.

And the Gerasene people? Oh, they probably just get new pigs, maybe even a new demoniac. Things probably just stay the same. . . . Or maybe, just maybe . . .

Looking for Likenesses in Contemporary African-American Poetry

After playing (both poetically and possessively) with the images in the story, we now go looking for likenesses to those images in contemporary African-American poetry. African Americans have historically been and remain U.S. scapegoats. They have experienced the violence of slavery, segregation, lynching, and discrimination. In these poems we hear the scapegoat dealing with violence. We hear images of pain, death, and hope.

I begin with a poem on the passage. Veronica Williams' unpublished "Haiku(s)" gives voice to the Gerasene:

Pain is all I feel
Ow! I just want to be healed
So, I ran and kneeled

The verb tenses are interesting here: the man has come to Jesus, but he's still feeling pain. Is he speaking to Jesus, hoping that Jesus can alleviate his pain and heal him? And exactly what pain is he talking about? The pain of the cuts he's inflicted on himself? The pain of isolation and depersonalization from the people? Williams seems to feel some of that pain herself. "Ow!" Is it the pain of being an African-American woman in this racist and sexist society? The poem is typewritten in a font that makes it appear like a child's handwriting. The Gerasene has regressed to a "wild child," giving vent to all the region's rage over Roman imperialism. Yet he is also the "identified child," the one deemed possessed when it is the entire region that is possessed by Rome.

Ruth-Miriam Garnett deals with the possession of contemporary violence in her poem "Concerning Violence," which is dedicated to Frantz Fanon. She says that "this war" gives "reasons for our madness." Dogma and mask take her people "noiselessly to burial." So they kill with bare hands. The poet concludes by saying that she has "two minds," one of which is the warden for the other.[28] The Roman imperial oppression, which eventually gave way to war, gave reason for the Gerasene's madness. He was delivered "noiselessly to burial," and he cut himself with his own bare hands. He had many more than two minds—a whole legion of them, and maybe one was the warden and others were guards (the pigs!).

Like the Gerasene, many poems by African Americans come "out of the tombs." Baba Lukata sees three African-American young men lying in a cemetery and he wonders if it is a "Rehearsal."[29] The poet is aware that African-American young men are an endangered species, and indeed, one or more of the three may be on the underside of that graveyard now. Also set in a cemetery, Ira B. Jones' poem "Alley Games 6 / The Ascension" hauntingly describes the funeral of a young man who was a victim of "an alley war game." His mother's eyes were "Dreary with the pain of prayers hung on a broken cross."[30] Indeed, it is the Markan Jesus who tells his disciples to deny themselves, take up their cross and follow him (8:34). What might that mean in the "'hood"?

---

[28] Ruth-Miriam Garnett, "Concerning Violence," in E. Ethelbert Miller, ed., *Beyond the Frontier: African American Poetry for the 21st Century* (Baltimore: Black Classic Press, 2002) 251.

[29] Baba Lukata, "Rehearsal," *Beyond the Frontier*, 252.

[30] Ira B. Jones, "Alley Games 6 / The Ascension," *Beyond the Frontier*, 253.

A "funeral grief song" also begins Mbali Umoja's anthemlike poem "Say Something: A Change Is Gonna Come," which speaks of "zombied hunters armed with self hatred and a gun," who "murder for fun." The poet asks "how many more" funerals, bodies, and dead boys there will be, for "we've cracked under the magnitude of it all." But the change that's gonna come involves love, that is, self-love, which will lead to healing and freedom.[31] Yes, the Gerasene cracked under the magnitude of it all. Crrracked. But his healing, his liberation, involved compassion that the Lord had on him (Mark 5:19), which doubtlessly enabled him to have compassion on himself.

Looking for Likenesses in My Own Soul

Where are the likenesses to the story's images in my own soul? I am most taken with the Gerasene U.S.man's self-inflicted violence: screaming and stone-cutting himself. SCREAMing and CUTting. I scream (inwardly) and I cut myself with stony words: "I hate myself." "I'm no good." "I want to die." It's the depression and anxiety speaking. They are the unclean spirits that invade my soul. Can I, however, harness clean, holy spirits to proclaim the good news: "I love myself." ("And a voice came out of the heavens, "You are my beloved child, in which I'm pleased," Mark 1:11). "I am good." "I want to live"?

I identify in this passage with the victim. In what ways am I the victimizer: the townspeople who scapegoat the man, and even the Romans, represented by the demonic legions, who maintain their privilege through violence? I am a white, male intellectual. How much more privileged can I be in our society? In what ways do I participate in the violence of this U.S. imperialistic society that scapegoats the poor, ethnic and racial minorities, and homosexuals? And how is this scapegoating violence in society at large reflected in the scapegoating violence I perpetrate in my own psyche? And in what ways do I resist both social and psychological scapegoating violence?

Soon after I agreed to write the essay that later became this chapter, I participated in a weekend, twenty-four-hour advanced Alternatives to Violence Project workshop at the Maryland Correctional Institution at Jessup, MD. (I had done the beginning workshop the year previously.)[32] During

---

[31] Mbali Umoja, "Say Something: A Change Is Gonna Come," *Beyond the Frontier,* 277–79.

[32] For information about the Alternatives to Violence Project (AVP) see the website of AVP-USA, *http://www.avpusa.org*. Incidentally, you will note that I dedicate this book to the men at the Maryland Correctional Institution and the women at the Maryland Correctional Institution for Women, both at Jessup, MD, who have participated in AVP.

this workshop I was struck with the stories of the men who told me about how prison life dehumanized them. One man told me during that hot July weekend how the prisoners sweltered in cells that were not air-conditioned. His roommate told me how he could extend his arms and touch facing walls. When one man asked me for information, I asked him if he had access to the Internet. He said, "Are you kidding? Of course not!" Another man said that if they wore shorts, they had to be of a certain length and of a certain gray color. He told me that a guard prohibited him from wearing a particular pair of shorts he had ordered from a mail-order company because the shorts were the wrong shade of gray!

With these stories and many more in mind, the day following the workshop I read Mark 5:1-20 and wrote this poem:

> they r
> they r
> da scapegoats
> uv r society
>
> da prisnrs
> our demons
> dey got
>
> our penaltiez
> r sins
> dey got
>
> stone m
> humiliate dm
> d / humnz m
>
> strip awa dere manhood   persnhood
> dis iz dere hood   now
> dere hood
> dere hood
>
> r scapegoats
> da prisnrs
>
> kil m
>
> n we kill   n imprisn   n d   humnz   r   selvs
>
> da chaind ls
>
> 2 wich we r chaind
>
> i dunno if i can evr reed da story   da same way   agn

he iz leejun
they r leejun
i m leejun

we all   ALL   r   leejn

Yes, yes. All of us. As long as we tolerate the dehumanization of the criminal (in)justice system, we are in a sick relationship with the state and with these prisoners, and we as a society and individuals are demon-possessed.

So how are we healed? How might we all come to a place in which we are, like the Gerasene, "seated, shirted, and sane"? Diagnosis is much easier than cure. I am tempted to list off a bunch of things, but I see on my office wall here my personal mission statement, and I think that it will be healing, at least for me, to include it here:

I believe
in humanity,
in the human individual in human community
in humanization, that is,
    nurturing all people
    so that they might become more and more human.

I believe
in my own humanity,
    which I nurture
    through meditation, through writing, through reading,
    through exercise, through creative expression such as poetry
        and art,
    and through living in community with my nuclear family:
    Joy, Anastasia, and Miranda Newheart.

I believe, then,
in my family's humanity,
    which is so bound up with mine.
    They humanize me as I humanize them,
    loving them, listening to them, supporting them, and encouraging
        them.
    My first priority is to Joy
    as we join together in raising this family as a witness to human
        community.

I believe, finally,
in the humanity of all persons,

which I serve professionally at Howard University School of
   Divinity
and ecclesiastically at Adelphi Friends Meeting,
joining with these groups to humanize the world,
promoting peace and justice, building community,
so that all people might be free.

So that all people might be free . . . of poverty, of oppression, of scapegoating, of violence.[33]

Before I conclude, I would like to comment about a troubling aspect
of the story of the Gerasene. Violence is finally resolved through violence,
indeed, divine violence. Yes, it is pigs that die, but they are stand-ins for
people, Romans specifically. Just as God drowned the Egyptians in the sea,
so will God terminate the Romans and their oppressive rule. We can be
nonviolent because God is ultimately violent. He (and this image of God is
certainly male) does our dirty work for us. He accepts our rage . . . and
vents it on our scapegoats. (It seems that Girard and others have missed
this point.) How healthy is that? Not for the victims and not for us, the
"victors." Actually, it sounds pretty passive-aggressive to me: we're pas-
sive, God's aggressive. We never accept our rage; we just pass it on to our
suffering servant, who sends suffering on those making us servants. Is
there an Alternative to divine Violence? If so, that's my Project. I'm already trying to arrange "workshops."

Conclusion

Upon waking one morning when I was finishing the original form of
this chapter, I felt anxious (I won't get it done on time, it won't be good
enough, yada yada yada), so I wrote two poems (entitled "breeth" and
"fear here: haiku," respectively), then I drew a picture on the computer (entitled "gerasene terror"), then I read the following passage in a book I've
been reading on artistic inspiration, entitled *The Demon and the Angel*:

> [The Spanish poet Federico Garcia] Lorca rejoiced in the impulsive
> fluidity of drawing, the sheer pleasure of making "senseless black
> strokes with the pen." . . . Drawing was for him a calmer haven, less

---

[33] In his most recent books Richard Horsley has considered the relevance of Jesus'
proclamation to "the new American empire." See his *Jesus and Empire: The Kingdom of
God and the New World Disorder* (Minneapolis: Fortress, 2003) and *Religion and Empire:
People, Power, and the Life of the Spirit* (Minneapolis: Fortress, 2004).

imperiled than writing, more grounded and harmonious. . . . Lorca felt that in making graphic art he had his feet planted firmly on the ground, which was not the case with writing, where he moved through fiercer and more abysmal ground and was sometimes lifted into stranger and more unknown dimensions. . . . The demons Lorca tended to keep at bay in his exuberant graphic art were released into his poems and plays, which are more desperately shadowed by death, and more fully become rites of exorcism.[34]

Has this poetic, playful exegesis been an exorcism for me? Has it been right? rite? write? Am I seated, shirted, and sane? Sane? Such a relative term, isn't it? Seated and shirted here, am I saner than before? I hope so. At least, more in touch with my (our?) insanity, which is surely a symptom of sanity.

I am certainly like the Decapolitans at the end of the story: I am amazed, uh-mazed, in a maze.

---

[34] Edward Hirsch, *The Demon and the Angel: Searching for the Source of Artistic Inspiration* (New York: Harcourt, 2002) 23.

CONCLUSION
Telling the Story, Enriching the Soul

So we've come to the end of our consideration of the Gerasene story. How do you feel? Maybe you feel like some of the characters in the story. Maybe you feel like the people of the Ten Cities, amazed? Maybe you feel like the Gerasenes, afraid? Or maybe you feel like the pigs, drowned? In the conclusion, we will try to tie up loose ends. Huh? You mean we're going to try to bind up the Gerasene? That didn't work in the story. Why do you think it's going to work now?

It probably won't. The question, though, is: Has the Gerasene been bound for you? Or has he kept breaking free from whatever chains and fetters we've used on him, whether narrative criticism or psychological biblical criticism? Let's summarize what we've talked about in this book and then discuss some of the broader issues concerning demon possession and exorcism.

Trying to Bind Him Up

We have looked at the Gerasene story from two different perspectives, first from the perspective of narrative criticism and then from the perspective of psychological criticism. Narrative criticism looks at the gospels as narratives. Following Seymour Chatman, narrative critics speak about real and implied author and readers, about narrator and narratee, and about plot, character, and setting. We first looked at the Gospel of Mark using the following plot statement:

> Jesus the Son of God works miracles, teaches, and calls disciples, yet in doing so he meets opposition, which leads to his being rejected and killed, but God raises him.

Miracle-working, then, is an important activity for Jesus in Mark. It is one important way that God's ruling has drawn near. The kind of miracles he does most often in Mark is exorcism, and the most detailed exorcism story is that of the Gerasene demoniac, which has been the focus of the book. This story is important to the ongoing plot of Mark because it represents the first action Jesus does "on the other side of the sea." The Gerasene, then, is drawn in bolder relief than any other healed person in the gospel.

Psychological biblical criticism focuses on the psychological issues raised by the text. Unlike narrative criticism, which is dominated by Chatman's model, psychological biblical criticism follows no one model. We have highlighted those models that work well with narrative criticism, that is, those that focus on the psychic issues either of the characters in the text or of the hearer/reader of the text. First, we dealt with the psychodynamic theorists, Sigmund Freud and Carl Jung. Critics who have followed Freudian footsteps have talked about the "uncanny" nature of the Gerasene story because it brings back repressed feelings of omnipotence. Critics working in the Jungian tradition speak of the Gerasene as a shadow figure, who brings up in readers unacknowledged parts of themselves. Second, we discussed two theorists not well known in biblical or psychological studies, René Girard and Frantz Fanon. Girard and Girardian biblical critics consider the Gerasene a "scapegoat" who bears the violence of his people. Fanon's fans among biblical interpreters have contended that when Jesus elicits the name Legion from the Gerasene and then exorcizes him, he is drawing back the veil of mystification that surrounds Roman imperialism. Finally, I set forth my own "soul reading" of the story, which poetically played with the powerful images of the story, found likenesses for those images in contemporary African-American poetry about violence, and looked for likenesses in my own soul.

So where are we? Better yet, where are you? What has happened to you as you've read this book, as you've read the Gospel of Mark, and as you've read the story of the Gerasene? I said in the introduction that I hoped you would be more critical, creative, and compassionate as a result of reading this book. In what ways has that happened?

Put the book down and write a half-page to a page about what you got out of this book. If you need them, here are some questions to help guide you: What is your understanding of narrative criticism? What does it add to your understanding of Mark's story of the Gerasene? What is your understanding of psychological biblical criticism? What does it add to your understanding of Mark's story of the Gerasene? How do these viewpoints help you read better? What do you see?

Gazing at the Gerasene, Then and Now

I said in the introduction that when I was teaching in college I would sometimes do a dramatic monologue of the Gerasene. I also said that I enjoyed this monologue so much I occasionally "took him on the road" when I was invited to preach in local Baptist churches. I remember one such occasion at First Baptist Church, Cape Girardeau, Missouri, which is the major city in the region of the state called "the Bootheel." I did the Gerasene monologue as the sermon for a Sunday evening worship service. After the sermon, when I was "shaking out" members of the congregation, the minister of education at the church, who was a recent seminary graduate, asked me whether I thought the man really had demons, or was he mentally ill? I don't remember my response. I do remember, though, that he wanted to pursue the topic with me, but there wasn't time or opportunity.

Maybe you have some of the same questions. Did the Gerasene really have demons or was he mentally ill? First of all, the event as it is narrated in the Gospel of Mark probably did not happen. It is highly unlikely that Jesus put demons into pigs, which rushed into the sea. The story is simply too fantastic. Perhaps some historical incident does lie behind it. Maybe Jesus exorcized a deeply disturbed man in Gentile territory, and before the gospel was written a preacher or teacher added to the story so that it would serve the preaching and teaching needs of the early church. Then Mark continued to elaborate the story so that it served the narrative purposes of his gospel.[1]

It is unquestionable that Jesus was regarded as an exorcist in his own day. He performed deeds that were interpreted as the exorcisms of demons. It seems that he encountered deeply disturbed people who were said to have demons, or unclean spirits. In Jesus' presence they experienced relief. Looking at some of these stories from the perspective of twenty-first-century medicine, we might "diagnose" these characters differently. For example, the young man whose father comes to Jesus and his disciples (Mark 9:14-29) seems to have epilepsy. And perhaps some demoniacs had what we would call multiple personality disorder. But really that is beside the point. The Gospel of Mark, as well as much of the New Testament, holds an apocalyptic worldview, which says that the world is now in an evil age dominated by the devil and his demons. Jesus heralds the coming of a new age characterized by the defeat of these evil powers, as shown in the exorcisms. We may not accept that worldview for our functioning in the

---

[1] For a similar view see John P. Meier, *A Marginal Jew: Rethinking the Historical Jesus* (New York: Doubleday, 1994) 2:650–53; Robert W. Funk and the Jesus Seminar, *The Acts of Jesus: What Did Jesus Really Do?* (San Francisco: HarperSanFrancisco, 1998) 78–79.

twenty-first century, but we must accept it for our reading of the Gospel of Mark. It is the way Jesus and his contemporaries coped with the desperate situation of Roman imperialism and its devastating effect on the individual and group psyche.

And it is a worldview many people today still find meaningful, even in the United States. Michael Cuneo in *American Exorcism: Expelling Demons in the Land of Plenty* documents some of the many exorcism and deliverance ministries that have risen to prominence in the last thirty years, since the publication of William Peter Blatty's *The Exorcist* and the film of the same name. Cuneo writes, "As unlikely as it may sound, exorcism is alive and well in contemporary America."[2] He continues, "Whatever one's personal problem—depression, anxiety, substance addiction, or even a runaway sexual appetite—there are exorcism ministries available today that will happily claim expertise for dealing with it."[3]

Cuneo deals mostly with those who are on the conservative side of the theological spectrum. While those on the liberal side mostly shy away from "demon" language, some use it to speak of social problems, such as materialism, militarism, and racism. Ched Myers includes in his book on Mark, *Say to This Mountain,* "A Psalm for Casting out Demons." Demons are identified as drugs, violence, envy, injustice, and war.[4] At an ecumenical prayer gathering immediately before Richard Nixon's second inauguration as president in 1973, activist William Stringfellow concluded his sermon with a prayer of exorcism, in which he implored God to free Nixon from demon possession. At the 1984 annual protest at the site where the first atomic bomb was tested, a Catholic priest administered a rite of exorcism for the nation's collective demon of the possession of nuclear weapons.[5]

Mark's apocalyptic language, then, is still with us. It should not be surprising, here at the beginning of the second millennium. Just as first-

---

[2] Michael W. Cuneo, *American Exorcism: Expelling Demons in the Land of Plenty* (New York: Doubleday, 2001) xii. Some of the literature he discusses includes Malachi Martin, *Hostage to the Devil: The Possession and Exorcism of Five Contemporary Americans* (New York: Reader's Digest Press, 1976; rev. ed. San Francisco: HarperSanFrancisco, 1992), M. Scott Peck, *People of the Lie: The Hope for Healing Human Evil* (New York: Touchstone, 1983), and Francis MacNutt, *Deliverance from Evil Spirits: A Practical Manual* (Grand Rapids: Chosen Books, 1995).

[3] Ibid. xiii.

[4] Ched Myers, et al., *Say to This Mountain: Mark's Story of Discipleship* (Maryknoll, NY: Orbis, 1996) 229–31. The psalm is taken from Miriam Therese Winter, *WomanWisdom: A Feminist Lectionary and Psalter* (New York: Crossroad, 1991).

[5] For more on both of these stories see Walter Wink, *Unmasking the Powers: The Invisible Forces that Determine Human Existence.* The Powers, vol. 2 (Philadelphia: Fortress, 1986) 66–67.

century Mediterraneans felt out of control with the violence of Roman imperialism and "mystified" their situation in terms of the devil and demons, so we twenty-first-century North Americans feel out of control with widespread violence and "mystify" our situation in the same way. And some individuals act out that loss of control through bizarre behavior, which others can only explain through the language of demons. So they exorcize the demons in the individual souls with the hope (sometimes unconscious, sometimes conscious) that somehow soon the demons might be gone from society at large.

We need people to be out of control so that we might be in control, or so that we might live with the illusion of control in this out-of-control world. The Gerasenes are everywhere. They are legion.

Conclusion to the Conclusion

I was a panelist at a workshop on gang violence at a conference several years ago at Howard Divinity School. I said that gang members were like the Gerasene demoniac in that they carried our projections. We think of them as violent, sexually promiscuous, and drug addicted, and often (though not always) they live out our projections by being violent, sexually promiscuous, and drug addicted. I encouraged the attendees, as they worked with gangs, to get in touch with, and lead their congregations, to get in touch with those projections. I ask you now: In what sense do urban gangs carry our projections? What other groups seem to be carrying our violent projections? In other words, who are the Gerasene demoniacs in our world today? You might flip through the pages of today's newspaper to identify some. You might even make a Gerasene collage.

Who is the Gerasene in you? Where does he grab you? Where does your story intersect with his? In what ways have you been living among the tombs? What ways help you be "seated, dressed, and sane"? Where do you project your violence? In what ways do you serve as scapegoat for others? Who are those people who serve as scapegoat for you? Maybe you want to draw a picture of the Gerasene within you or write a song or poem about him. (Each time I have worked with this story, I have read it aloud and then I have often written a poem or drawn a sketch. See the Appendix for a few of my poems and some by my students.) Sometimes our creative faculties are more adept at accessing the hidden parts of ourselves than our intellectual faculties.

The Gerasene has become my "bosom buddy" in the last several months since I've been working on this book in earnest. I have called him "Gery" (pronounced like "Gary"). I hope that he has become your friend, too. He's quite a guy, and he's been through a lot. He's helped me name some of my own individual demons and our social demons. Thanks. Peace be with you, Gery. And also with you.

BIBLIOGRAPHY

Alter, Robert. *The Art of Biblical Narrative*. New York: Basic Books, 1981.

Bailie, Gil. *Violence Unveiled: Humanity at the Crossroads*. New York: Crossroad, 1995.

Berger, Klaus. *Identity and Experience in the New Testament*. Minneapolis: Fortress, 2003.

Bible and Culture Collective, The. *The Postmodern Bible*. New Haven: Yale University Press, 1995.

Bourguignon, Erika. *Possession*. Chandler & Sharp Series in Cross-Cultural Themes. San Francisco: Chandler & Sharp, 1976.

Capps, Donald. *Jesus: A Psychological Biography*. St. Louis: Chalice, 2000.

Carter, Warren. *Matthew and the Margins: A Sociopolitical and Religious Reading*. Maryknoll, NY: Orbis, 2000.

Chatman, Seymour. *Story and Discourse: Narrative Structure in Fiction and Film*. Ithaca, NY: Cornell University Press, 1978.

Clarke, John Henrik, ed. *Black American Short Stories: One Hundred Years of the Best*. New York: Hill and Wang, 1993.

Cuneo, Michael W. *American Exorcism: Expelling Demons in the Land of Plenty*. New York: Doubleday, 2001.

Davies, Stevan L. *Jesus the Healer: Possession, Trance, and the Origins of Christianity*. New York: Continuum, 1995.

Detweiler, Robert, and William G. Doty, eds. *The Daemonic Imagination*. American Academy of Religion Studies in Religion 60. Atlanta: Scholars, 1990.

Dols, William L. *Awakening the Fire Within: A Primer on Issue-Centered Education*. St. Louis: The Educational Center, 1994.

Donahue, John R., and Daniel J. Harrington. *The Gospel of Mark*. SP 2. Collegeville: Liturgical Press, 2002.

Dowd, Sharyn Echols. *Reading Mark: A Literary and Theological Commentary on the Second Gospel*. Macon, GA: Smyth & Helwys, 2000.

Fanon, Frantz. *Black Skin, White Masks*. Trans. Charles Lam Markmann. New York: Grove Press, 1967.

_____. *The Wretched of the Earth*. Trans. Constance Farrington. New York: Grove Press, 1963.

Felman, Shoshana, ed. *Literature and Psychoanalysis: The Question of Reading: Otherwise*. Baltimore: The Johns Hopkins University Press, 1982.

111

Girard, René. *The Scapegoat*. Trans. Yvonne Freccero. Baltimore: The Johns Hopkins University Press, 1986.

Grieb, A. Katherine. *The Story of Romans: A Narrative Defense of God's Righteousness*. Louisville: Westminster John Knox, 2002.

Hamerton-Kelly, Robert G. *The Gospel and the Sacred: Poetics of Violence in Mark*. Minneapolis: Fortress, 1994.

Hendricks, Obery. *Living Water: A Novel*. San Francisco: HarperSanFrancisco, 2003.

Hillman, James. *Revisioning Psychology*. New York: Harper & Row, 1975.

_____. "Further Notes on Images." *Spring* 40 (1978) 152–82.

_____. "Image-Sense." *Spring* 41 (1979) 130–43.

Hirsch, Edward. *The Demon and the Angel: Searching for the Source of Artistic Inspiration*. New York: Harcourt, 2002.

Hollenbach, Paul W. "Jesus, Demoniacs, and Public Authorities: A Socio-Historical Study." *Journal of the American Academy of Religion* 99 (1981) 567–88.

_____. "Help for Interpreting Jesus' Exorcisms." *Society of Biblical Literature Seminar Papers* 32. Atlanta: Scholars, 1993.

Horsley, Richard A. *Hearing the Whole Story: The Politics of Plot in Mark's Gospel*. Louisville: Westminster John Knox, 2001.

Hughes, Langston, ed. *The Best Short Stories by Black Writers: The Classic Anthology from 1899 to 1967*. New York: Little, Brown, 1967.

Jacobi, Jolande. *The Psychology of C. G. Jung*. New Haven: Yale University Press, 1973.

Juel, Donald H. A *Master of Surprise: Mark Interpreted*. Minneapolis: Fortress, 1994.

Jung, Carl Gustav. *The Collected Works of C. G. Jung*. Herbert Read, Michael Fordham and Gerhard Adler, eds. 20 vols. Bollingen Series 20. Princeton: Princeton University Press, 1966–79.

Kahn, Michael. *Basic Freud: Psychoanalytic Thought for the 21st Century*. New York: Basic Books, 2002.

Keegan, Terence J. *Interpreting the Bible: A Popular Introduction to Biblical Hermeneutics*. New York: Paulist, 1985.

Kelber, Werner H. *Mark's Story of Jesus*. Philadelphia: Fortress, 1979.

Kille, D. Andrew. *Psychological Biblical Criticism*. Guides to Biblical Scholarship: Old Testament Series. Minneapolis: Fortress, 2001.

Kingsbury, Jack Dean. *Conflict in Mark: Jesus, Authorities, Disciples*. Minneapolis: Fortress, 1989.

Lacan, Jacques. *Écrits: A Selection*. Trans. Alan Sheridan. New York: Norton, 1977.

MacNutt, Francis. *Deliverance from Evil Spirits: A Practical Manual*. Grand Rapids: Chosen Books, 1995.

Malbon, Elizabeth Struthers. *Hearing Mark: A Listener's Guide*. Harrisburg, PA: Trinity Press International, 2002.

_____. *In the Company of Jesus: Characters in Mark's Gospel*. Louisville: Westminster John Knox, 2000.

_____. "Narrative Criticism: How Does the Story Mean?" in Janice Capel Anderson and Stephen Moore, eds., *Mark and Method*. Minneapolis: Fortress, 1992, 23–49.

McGann, Diarmuid. *The Journeying Self: The Gospel of Mark through a Jungian Perspective*. New York: Paulist, 1985.

_____. *Journeying Within Transcendence: The Gospel of John through a Jungian Perspective*. New York: Paulist, 1988.

Martin, Malachi. *Hostage to the Devil: The Possession and Exorcism of Five Contemporary Americans*. Rev. ed. San Francisco: HarperSanFrancisco, 1992.

McMillan, Terry, ed. *Breaking Ice: An Anthology of Contemporary African-American Fiction*. New York: Penguin, 1990.

Merenlahti, Petri. *Poetics for the Gospels? Rethinking Narrative Criticism*. Studies of the New Testament and Its World. London: T & T Clark, 2002.

_____. "Reading Mark for the Pleasure of Fantasy." in J. H. Ellens and W. G. Rollins, eds., *Psychology and the Bible: A New Way to Read Scriptures*. Westport, CT: Praeger, forthcoming.

Miller, E. Ethelbert, ed. *Beyond the Frontier: African American Poetry for the 21st Century*. Baltimore: Black Classic Press, 2002.

Moore, Stephen D. *Literary Criticism and the Gospels: The Theoretical Challenge*. New Haven: Yale University Press, 1989.

_____. *Mark and Luke in Poststructuralist Perspective: Jesus Begins to Write*. New Haven: Yale University Press, 1992.

Newheart, Michael Willett. "Johannine Symbolism," in David L. Miller, ed., *Jung and the Interpretation of the Bible*. New York: Continuum, 1995, 71–91. Reprinted as "The Psychology of Johannine Symbolism," in J. H. Ellens and W. G. Rollins, eds., *Psychology and the Bible: A New Way to Read Scriptures*. Westport, CT: Praeger, forthcoming.

_____. "Toward a Psycho-Literary Reading of the Fourth Gospel," in Fernando F. Segovia, ed., *"What is John? " Readers and Readings of the Fourth Gospel*. Society of Biblical Literature Symposium Series 3. Atlanta: Scholars, 1996, 43–58.

_____. "The Soul of the Father and the Son: A Psychological (yet Playful and Poetic) Approach to the Father-Son Language in the Fourth Gospel," *Semeia: Experimental Journal of Biblical Criticism* 85 (1999) 155–75.

_____. "Soul 2 Soul: A Post-Modern Exegete in Search of (New Testament) Soul," *Journal of Religious Thought* 55.2–56.1 (2000) 1–17.

_____. *Word and Soul: A Psychological, Literary, and Cultural Reading of the Fourth Gospel*. Collegeville: The Liturgical Press, 2001.

Pasteur, Alfred B., and Ivory L. Toldson. *Roots of Soul: The Psychology of Black Expressiveness*. Garden City, NY: Doubleday, 1982.

Petersen, Norman R. *Literary Criticism for New Testament Critics*. Guides to Biblical Scholarship: New Testament Series. Philadelphia: Fortress, 1978.

Powell, Mark Allen. *Chasing the Eastern Star: Adventures in Reader-Response Criticism*. Louisville: Westminster John Knox, 2001.

_____. *The Bible and Modern Literary Criticism: A Critical and Annotated Bibliography.* Westport, CT: Greenwood Press, 1992.

_____. "Toward a Narrative-Critical Understanding of Mark." *Interpretation* 47/4 (October 1993) 341–46.

_____. *What Is Narrative Criticism?* Guides to Biblical Scholarship: New Testament Series. Minneapolis: Fortress, 1990.

Reiser, Lynn. *Cherry Pies and Lullabies.* New York: Greenwillow Books, 1998.

Rhoads, David. "Jesus and the Syrophoenician Woman in Mark. A Narrative-Critical Study." *Journal of the American Academy of Religion* 62 (1994) 343–75.

_____. "Narrative Criticism and the Gospel of Mark." *Journal of the American Academy of Religion* 50 (1982) 411–34.

_____, Joanna Dewey, and Donald Michie. *Mark as Story: An Introduction to the Narrative of a Gospel.* 2nd ed. Minneapolis: Fortress, 1999.

_____, and Kari Syreeni, eds. *Characterization in the Gospels: Reconceiving Narrative Criticism.* Journal for the Study of the New Testament Supplement Series 184. Sheffield: Sheffield Academic Press, 1999.

Ricci, Nino. *Testament.* Boston: Houghton Mifflin, 2003.

Rollins, Wayne G. *Jung and the Bible.* Atlanta: John Knox, 1983.

_____. *Soul and Psyche: The Bible in Psychological Perspective.* Minneapolis: Fortress, 1999.

Schaer, Hans. *Religion and the Cure of Souls in Jung's Psychology.* Trans. R.F.C. Hull. Bollingen Series XXI. New York: Pantheon Books, 1950.

Smith, Stephen H. *A Lion With Wings: A Narrative-Critical Approach to Mark's Gospel.* Sheffield: Sheffield Academic Press, 1996.

Starobinski, Jean. "An Essay in Literary Analysis—Mark 5:1-20." *Ecumenical Review* 23 (1971) 377–97.

_____. "The Gerasene Demoniac," in Roland Barthes, ed., *Structural Analysis and Biblical Exegesis.* Pittsburgh: Pickwick, 1974, 57–84.

Stein, Murray. *Jung's Map of the Soul: An Introduction.* Chicago: Open Court, 1998.

Stirling, Mack C. "Violent Religion: René Girard's Theory of Culture," in J. Harold Ellens, ed., *The Destructive Power of Religion: Violence in Judaism, Christianity, and Islam.* Westport, CT: Praeger, 2004, 11–50.

Storr, Anthony. *Freud.* Past Masters. Oxford: Oxford University Press, 1989.

Tannehill, Robert C. "The Gospel of Mark as Narrative Christology." *Semeia* 16 (1979) 57–95.

Theissen, Gerd. *Psychological Aspects of Pauline Theology.* Philadelphia: Fortress, 1987.

_____. *The Shadow of the Galilean: The Quest of the Historical Jesus in Narrative Form.* Philadelphia: Fortress, 1987.

Tolbert, Mary Ann. "How the Gospel of Mark Builds Character." *Interpretation* 47/4 (October 1993) 347–57.

_____. "Introduction and Annotations to the Gospel According to Mark," in Walter J. Harrelson, ed., *The New Interpreter's Study Bible.* Nashville: Abingdon, 2003, 1801–45.

_____. *Sowing the Gospel: Mark's World in Literary-Historical Perspective.* Minneapolis: Fortress, 1989.

Tompkins, Jane P., ed. *Reader-Response Criticism: From Formalism to Post-Structuralism.* Baltimore: The Johns Hopkins University Press, 1980.

Uleyn, Arnold J. R. "The Possessed Man of Gerasa: A Psychoanalytic Interpretation of Reader Reactions," in J. van Belzen and Jan van der Lans, eds., *Current Issues in the Psychology of Religion: Proceedings of the Third Symposium on the Psychology of Religion in Europe.* Amsterdam: Rodopi, 1986, 90–96.

_____. "A Psychoanalytic Approach to Mark's Gospel." *Lumen Vitae* 32 (1977) 479–93.

Wallace, Mark I., and Theophus H. Smith, eds. *Curing Violence.* Forum Fascicles. Sonoma, CA: Polebridge, 1994.

Ward, Colleen A., and Michael H. Beaubrun. "The Psychodynamics of Demon Possession." *Journal for the Scientific Study of Religion* 19/2 (1980) 201–207.

Willett, Michael E. "Jung and John." *Explorations: Journal for Adventurous Thought* (Fall 1988) 77–92.

_____. *Wisdom Christology in the Fourth Gospel.* San Francisco: Mellen Research University Press, 1992.

Williams, James G. *The Bible, Violence, and the Sacred: Liberation from the Myth of Sanctioned Violence.* New York: HarperCollins, 1991.

Williams, Joel F. *Other Followers of Jesus: Minor Characters as Major Figures in Mark's Gospel.* Journal for the Study of the New Testament Supplement Series 102. Sheffield: JSOT Press, 1994.

Wink, Walter. *The Bible in Human Transformation: Toward a New Paradigm for Biblical Study.* Philadelphia: Fortress, 1973.

_____. *Transforming Bible Study: A Leader's Guide.* Nashville: Abingdon, 1980, 1989.

_____. *Engaging the Powers: Discernment and Resistance in a World of Domination.* The Powers, vol. 3. Minneapolis: Fortress, 1992.

_____. *Unmasking the Powers: The Invisible Forces that Determine Human Existence.* The Powers, vol. 2. Philadelphia: Fortress, 1986.

Poems on the Gerasene

My Poems (unedited)

gerasene pigs (mark 5:11-13)

oink   oink   oink
          oink   oink
OINK   OINK   OINK
OINKOINKOINKOINKOINKOINKOINKOINK
kersplash!
glub   glub   glub
     glub   glub
     glub

062102

gery tanka

who r u n me, gery
n me wher do u dwel
among wat tombs
where do i heer ur screams
wher do i feel ur stones

100602

gery 2 jezus

highest godz holy blovd spirted son
u got da powa
2 pow doze demns
rite outa me
pow m gud
n it wil b gud

gud nuz
da kingdm

061102

legion haiku

my name is legion
six thousand voices calling
which one will i heed

untitled

marvelmarvel   i marvel 2
@ jesus man pigs
run cut screem heal drown
wata a scene garish scene
deres marvelus powr heer

102302

untitled

must i bcum d dmoniac
n ord 2 rite dis bk
iz der ini udr wa

giv myself ovr 2 d madnes
d cutn howln chainbrekn dmn

i giv mysef 2 u
i ofr my bod as a
livn
sacrifice

chain me

22jul03

mY naMe is lEgiOn
fOR wE aRe MaNy mAnY maNY **MAny** manY MANy MANY many
mANY Many mAny MaNY mANy MaNy mAnY maNY MANy manY
MANy MANY many mANY Many mAny MaNY mANy MaNy mAnY maNY
MAny manY MANy MANY many mANY Many mAny MaNY *mANy*
MaNy mAnY **maNY MAny** manY MANy MANY many mANY Many

mAny MaNY mANy MaNy mAnY maNY MAny manY MANy MANY
many mANY Many mAny MaNY mANy **MaNy** mAnY maNY MAny
manY MANy MANY many mANY Many mAny MaNY mANy MaNy
mAnY maNY MAny manY MANy MANY many mANY Many mAny
MaNY mANy MaNy mAnY maNY MAny manY MANy MANY *many*
mANY Many mAny MaNY mANy MaNy mAnY maNY MAny manY
MANy MANY many mANY Many mAny MaNY mANy MaNy mAnY
maNY *MAny* manY MANy MANY many mANY Many mAny MaNY
mANy MaNy mAnY maNY MAny manY MANy MANY many mANY
Many mAny MaNY mANy MaNy mAnY maNY MAny manY MANy
MANY many mANY Many mAny MaNY mANy MaNy mAnY maNY
MAny manY MANy MANY many mANY Many mAny MaNY mANy
MaNy mAnY maNY MAny manY MANy MANY many mANY Many
mAny MaNY mANy MaNy mAnY maNY MAny manY *MANy MANY*
many mANY Many mAny MaNY mANy MaNy mAnY maNY MAny
manY MANy MANY many mANY Many mAny MaNY mANy MaNy
mAnY maNY MAny manY MANy MANY *many mANY Many* mAny
MaNY mANy MaNy mAnY maNY MAny manY MANy MANY many
mANY Many mAny **MaNY** mANy MaNy mAnY maNY MAny manY
MANy MANY many mANY Many mAny MaNY mANy MaNy mAnY
maNY MAny manY MANy MANY many mANY Many mAny MaNY
mANY MaNY mANY manY MAny manY MANy MANY many mANY
Many mAny MaNY mANy MaNy mAnY maNY MAny manY MANy
MANY many mANY Many mAny MaNY mANy MaNy mAnY maNY
MAny manY MANy MANY many mANY Many mAny MaNY mANy
MaNy mAnY maNY MAny manY MANy MANY many mANY Many
mAny MaNY mANy MaNy mAnY maNY MAny manY MANy MANY
many mANY Many mAny MaNY mANy MaNy mAnY maNY MAny
manY MANy MANY many mANY Many mAny MaNY mANy MaNy
mAnY maNY MAny manY MANy MANY many mANY Many mAny
MaNY mANy MaNy mAnY maNY MAny manY MANy MANY many
mANY Many mAny MaNY mANy MaNy mAnY maNY MAny manY
MANy MANY many mANY Many mAny MaNY mANy MaNy mAnY
maNY MAny manY MANy MANY many mANY Many mAny MaNY
mANy MaNy mAnY maNY MAny manY MANy MANY many mANY
Many mAny MaNY mANy

(undated)

Song

chorus

seateddressed sane   ok
seated dressed sane   ok
seated dressed sane   ok

d man had a demon
no a legion a demons

chorus

but jezus cast m out
jezus cast m out

chorus

n2 d pigs   n d pigs n d c
n d c & drownd

corus

d peepl wr scared
wat wr dey fraid a

corus

so d man goz a preechn
& peepl wr amazd

corus

(undated)

Haiku Written by My Introduction to New Testament I Class, Fall 2003

Bound with misery
Now I walk in liberty
Jesus set me free

    —Guy Robinson

unsettling fear
thrashing, raging, possessed man
unsettling peace

    —Allison Ranta

Was I a demon?
You asked my name, hark
The healing began

　　—Diana D. Gomez de Molina

From Tombs of darkness and strife
He rescued me that very dreary night
Jesus Christ renewed my life.

　　—George C. Brown

Man cries for release
Needing the turmoil to cease
In Jesus finds peace

　　—Sabrina Mangrum

How do I presume
Legion to be different
From who I am now?

　　—Marcia Price

Bound by oppression
Desiring to be loosed
Freed by God's mercy

　　—Sabrina Malachi

Possessed one in chains,
Jesus made you free indeed.
Go and tell the world.

　　—Rodney Teal

Devils are in me
Master come and set me free
Yes, there are many

　　—Miriam Wright

SCRIPTURE INDEX

Genesis
ch. 2–3   57
22:2   19, 31

Exodus
15:1-10   84
19:3-25   27
20:12   25

Leviticus
11:7-8   45
21:1   42
22:4-5   42

Deuteronomy
5:16   25
14:1   43
14:8   45

Psalms
2:7   19
22   31
22:1   32
22:1-21a   32
22:7   31
22:18   31
22:21b-31   32
42:7   89
69:21   31

Isaiah
6:9-10   25
40:3   25
42:1   19
65:4   42, 45

Daniel
7:14   26

Matthew
ch. 1–2   17
1:18–2:12   14
5:3-12   5
5:20   6
6:9-15   5
8:28-34   xxi, 16
10:5-6   6
14:22-33   55
14:33   20
15:21-28   16
16:16   20
20:29-34   16
23:13-36   16
26:6-13   16
28:20   6

Mark
1:1   41, 48, 93, 95
1:2-3   25, 31
1:3   47
1:4   98
1:7   47
1:9-10   93
1:9-11   5
1:9   14, 19
1:10-12   94
1:10   21, 32, 93, 94
1:11   31, 32, 95, 100
1:12   21
1:13   31, 95

1:14-15   24, 26
1:14   47, 98
1:14–8:21   34
1:15   27
1:16-20   26, 41, 93
1:16   93
1:18   21
1:21–2:12   21, 26, 35
1:21-28   20, 24, 37, 42, 93, 94
1:21-23   94
1:22   22, 23
1:23   21, 37, 38, 42
1:24   38, 43, 44, 95
1:25   21, 36, 38, 44
1:26   37, 43, 44
1:27   22, 23, 27, 37, 47
1:29-31   21, 94
1:29   21
1:31   31
1:32-34   21
1:32-33   21, 42
1:34   22, 44, 93
1:39   21, 42, 93
1:40-45   21, 93
1:41-42   21, 94
1:42   42
1:43-45   22
1:44-45   33
1:44   46, 98
1:45   47
2:1-12   21, 23, 93

2:5-12	23	4:10	25	5:37	27
2:9	23	4:11-12	28	5:39	39
2:10-11	22	4:11	27, 35, 93	5:41	25, 32
2:11	46	4:12	25	5:42	39
2:12	22, 23, 42, 47	4:33-34	35	6:2-3	30
2:13-14	93	4:34	27	6:5-6	30
2:13	41	4:35-41	24, 27, 35, 36,	6:7-13	27, 35, 93
2:13–3:6	35		41, 93	6:12	47
2:15-17	93	4:35	41	6:30-44	24, 35
2:15	26	4:36	42	6:30-43	24
2:16	23	4:37-38	42	6:45-52	24, 28, 35
2:18–3:6	27	4:37	43, 44	6:46	43
2:18-21	23	4:38	94	6:47-52	93
2:23-28	23	4:40-41	37, 46	6:51	47
2:28	22	4:41	93, 97	7:1-23	35
3:1-6	23	5:1-20	xix–xx, 16, 20,	7:5	25
3:4	23		24, 35, 89, 101	7:11	25, 32
3:5-6	28	5:1	41	7:17	27
3:6	23, 30, 31, 42	5:2	37, 38, 42, 94	7:19	26
3:7-12	21	5:3-5	13	7:24-29	35
3:7	27, 41	5:3-4	42, 43, 94	7:24-30	16, 20, 24, 26,
3:9	42	5:3	42, 43, 94		37
3:11-12	22	5:4	43	7:27	94
3:11	20, 42, 43, 44,	5:5	37, 39, 43, 94	7:34	25, 32
	93, 95	5:6	37, 38	7:36	33, 46, 47
3:13-19	27, 35	5:7	37, 38, 47	7:37	47
3:13-19a	93	5:8	38	8:1-10	24, 35
3:13-15	97	5:9	41, 44	8:14-20	28
3:13	27, 43	5:10	41, 45, 97	8:14-21	24, 35, 93
3:14	46, 98	5:12	39, 41, 97	8:22-26	28, 93
3:16-17	44	5:13	38	8:22–15:47	34
3:16	95	5:14	45	8:22–10:52	23
3:19b-35	24	5:15	xxi, 37, 38, 39,	8:27–9:1	28
3:19	27, 31		45	8:29-33	32
3:21	30	5:18-20	38	8:29-31	20
3:22-30	21	5:18	42	8:31-33	93
3:26-27	95	5:19	100	8:31	20
3:27	43, 48, 95	5:20	37	8:34	20, 31, 99
3:31-35	30	5:21-45	24	8:34	31
3:34-35	35	5:21-43	36	9:2	27
4:1–10:52	78	5:25-34	98	9:3	45
4:1–6:56	78	5:26	42	9:7	20
4:1-34	25, 35, 93	5:33	37	9:14-29	20, 37, 107
4:1	41, 42, 94	5:34	28, 37	9:15	47
4:2	42	5:36	37, 46	9:17	37

9:18	39	13:35	26
9:20	39	13:37	26
9:21	39	14:1	30
9:22	39, 43, 95	14:3-9	16
9:25	37, 38, 44	14:12-31	29
9:26-27	39	14:28	32
9:26	37, 38, 43	14:32-42	29
9:28	27	14:33	27
9:29	37	14:36	32
9:30-37	28	14:38-40	40
9:30-32	93	14:43	30
9:30	32	14:49-50	29
9:38-50	29	14:50	30, 93
9:38	44	14:51	46
10:10-11	27	14:53-65	30
10:13-16	29	15:1-15	16
10:17-22	16	15:1	30
10:32-45	29	15:5	47, 98
10:32-40	93	15:15-20	30
10:32	47	15:21-41	31
10:33-34	30, 32	15:21	31
10:45-52	28, 93	15:23	31
10:46-52	16, 98	15:24	31
10:47-48	47, 98	15:29	31
10:50	45	15:31	31
10:52	47	15:32	32
11:9	47	15:33	31
11:12-25	24	15:34	32, 44
11:21	39	15:37	44
12:11	47	15:38	32
12:17	47	15:39	32, 93, 95
12:29-30	47	15:41	31
12:36	47	15:47	31
12:37	47	16:5	45, 47
13:1-37	26	16:7-8	47
13:2	32	16:7	29
13:10	98	16:8	29
13:20	47	16:9-20	30

Luke	
ch. 1–2	17
1:1-4	13
1:26-38	14
2:8-20	14
3:21-22	5
4:14-21	15
4:14	6
6:12	5
6:20-23	5
7:36-50	16
8:26-39	xxi
9:29	5
10:21	6
10:38-42	17
11:1	5
11:2-4	5

John	
1:1	14
1:14	14
3:1-21	17
4:7-42	17
5:1-18	17
11:1-44	17
20:1-18	17
20:31	12

Acts	
1:1-2	13
16:10-17	13
20:5-15	13
21:1-18	13
27:1–28:16	13

2 Corinthians	
12:7	55